A Journey in the Back Country

In the Winter of 1853-4

By

Frederick Law Olmsted

Author of "A Journey in the Seaboard Slave States," "A Journey in Texas,"
"Walks and Talks of an American Farmer in England," etc.

[Originally Issued in 1860]

In Two Volumes

Volume II

G. P. Putnam's Sons

New York   London
27 and 29 W. 23d Street   24 Bedford Street, Strand

The Knickerbocker Press

1907

CONTENTS

IN

THE BACK COUNTRY

CHAPTER VI—(*Continued*)

THE HIGHLANDERS

Ashville, July 11th.—This is a beautiful place among the hills, with a number of pretty country-seats about it, which, I suppose are summer residences of South Carolina planters. A great many of these "Southerners," as they are called here, are now travelling farther north, to spend the heat of summer at the numerous sulphur springs and other pleasure haunts, where good boarding-houses have been established for them along the cool region of the Blue Ridge. I passed one of these, a sulphur spring, yesterday. It was a white, wooden building, with a long piazza for smokers, loungers, and flirters, and a bowling alley and shuffle-board; with coaches and trotting wagons at the stable; poor women picking blackberries, poor men bringing fowls, schoolgirls studiously climbing romantic rocks and otherwise making themselves as pretty as possible, children fighting their black nurses,

and old gold spectacles stopping me to inquire if I was the mail, and if I had not got a newspaper.

It is very odd, by the way, what old news one keeps getting in these places far from telegraphs. I inquired here for a late paper, and the clerk of the hotel went to a store to get one. It was the *Ashville News*, with the same articles copied from New York papers, which I had read a month before. All this country is to be netted by railroads soon, however; that is, as soon as they can be built after an appropriation to assist them passes Congress. I have crossed engineers' stakes every day, I believe, since I left Jackson, Mississippi, and generally, when I stop at night, the farmer tells me that a railroad, which will be *the* link which is wanting, either in a direct communication between the Atlantic and the Mississippi, or between New York and New Orleans, is to pass between his house and his corn-crib, and that in consequence land about him has lately become of great value, that is, from four to ten dollars an acre. He is in great perplexity, too, to conclude how much he can make the railroad company pay for damages.

Day before yesterday I ascended "Balsam Mountain," said to have been recently ascertained to be the highest peak of the Appalachian chain. A barometrical measurement of Professor W. D. Jones, of Tennessee, makes it ten thousand and three hundred feet above the sea, or one hundred and five feet higher than Black Mountain, which has always had the reputation of being the highest. I was told that the ascent was

easy, and could be made on horseback to within less
than a quarter of a mile of the top. I was offered a
guide, but preferred to go alone, leaving Belshazzar to
rest and recruit below.

The mountain is one of a very lofty range, and the
gap between it and the next peak is crossed by a (State)
turnpike road. The distance to the top from this road is
about four miles, and its elevation above the road, four
thousand feet. A very rank growth of weeds and grass
covers the ground on nearly all parts of the mountain
to the top, which is all used as a range for cattle,
horses, and hogs, and would be very profitably employed in this way but for the havoc committed on
young cattle, and especially on swine and sheep,
by bears, wolves, and panthers.

The horses and cattle make so many paths that I
was soon led astray from the one which leads directly
to the top (if there is any such), and had to shape my
course by the sun, and the apparent feasibility of the
ground in different directions before me. The mountain, to within less than a mile from the top, is entirely
shaded by a forest of large trees, the chestnut predomi-
nating. The only change found as you ascend, is in
their height ; the trunks continually becoming shorter
and sturdier. At perhaps half a mile from the summit,
the trees appear gradually more scattered ; at length
there is a nearly bald zone, covered, however, with
grass and weeds waist high. Above this, at a quarter
of a mile from the top, begins a forest of balsam firs
(popularly called "balsams"). In the interval, be-

tween the two forests, the ascent was steep and
fatiguing. Whether owing to the exertion of climbing altogether, or somewhat to the rarity of the atmos-
phere, I was obliged to stop frequently to rest, to relieve
myself from a rush of blood to the head. The moment
I entered the balsam forest, I was freed from this.
These balsams are thirty or forty feet high, and under
their shelter flourish a variety of smaller trees and
shrubs. A great many of these trees have fallen
down, and the nearer I came to the top the steeper
became the ascent, the more frequent the prostrate
trees, and the thicker and more impenetrable the undergrowth, a large part of it being blackberry briars.
I crept under and climbed over, and pulled myself
along slowly, and at length came to a knob or pinnacle, across and upon which, trees and shrubs, and
stumps, with the roots uppermost, seemed to have
been hurled by a whirlwind. Supposing this to be
the summit itself, I climbed among the roots and
briars, the best way I could, until I got my head
above the wreck. It was very dark from the shade
of the standing trees, and I perceived that the rocks
rose still higher beyond. I worked my way down
again and continued climbing, until I reached a comparatively level surface of several yards in extent, from
which a number of trees had been cut away so as to
open a view in two or three directions. A dense cloud
hung in a circle all around the peak, and though it was
quite clear in the centre where I stood, I could not see
beyond it at all. Overhead, at a still vast apparent dis-

tance, were striæ, through which, at length, the sun came out for a few minutes, but the only effect was to give the cumulus below me a more mist-like and steamy appearance. At length came a slight breeze, and set it in rapid motion, and rent and lifted, and lowered it, so that I got a few glimpses across the neighboring mountains, and saw their tops rising above rolling thunder heads, one of which was dark, and probably discharging rain. I heard thunder, and conjectured that at a distance, the cloud within which I stood would appear to be a thunder cloud, woolly and snowy, and gilded when the sun shone, and dark and rainy below.

The peculiarity of this mountain-top, distinguishing it from all others I know, of nearly equal height, is its moderate temperature and consequent abundant vegetation. It was so warm (it was half past one), that, heated as I became on my exertions, I felt no necessity for putting on my coat. The air was soft and agreeable. The ground, a dark, rich soil, with rocks protruding and shaly stones, bore luxuriant coarse herbage. Beside the thick growth of firs, I noticed black birch, chestnut, mountain ash, wild currant, whortleberry, blackberry, honeysuckle, and a variety of cherry, all growing on the highest point. The air was of course moist, and everything damp, and this was evidently its usual condition. All the dead and broken-down trees and the rocks were covered thickly with mosses and lichens, which were charged with water like a soaked sponge.

I remained half an hour, hoping the cloud would clear away, but it only grew denser and darker. Beginning to descend, I found a path and endeavored to follow it, but as it soon ran into forks, branching out in every direction, I determined to pursue a direct course down the mountain to the edge of the balsam forest, and then follow its lower line until I came to the path, or to the ridge along which I knew the path or way usually followed, led. I got lost, however, in the cloud and descended at a point where the lower forest extended up so as to meet the firs. I could not see out, but turning to the left, continued descending diagonally. The slope was very steep, and the ground covered with shelving stones, so that it was difficult to keep my feet. At length, on an inclination of about thirty-five degrees, I slipped, caught myself with a quick motion of my foot, but at the next step, tripped on a protruding root or tangle of weeds, balanced for a moment and was then thrown down headlong. I was severely bruised, and for some minutes could not rise. Fortunately, at no great distance, I found a deep gully with a stream of cold water ; after bathing in which, I entirely recovered my strength, though it was not till after several days that the contusions I received ceased to be inconvenient. I soon reached a more moderate slope, with a rich soil, bearing large trees, and very luxuriant tangled herbage.

Meanwhile the cloud on the pinnacle was muttering thunder, and growing darker and more threatening. As I hastened on, I saw at no great distance, waddling

off through the weeds, two black bears, but was so fortunate as to meet no snakes, and nothing else at all memorable. At about half past six I reached the foot of the mountain, and shortly afterward the cloud on its summit swept downward and onward with heavy thunder and copious rain.

I was about five hours descending and reaching the house whence I started. The farmer said that he went nearly to the top to salt his cattle once a week, and he could go up and back again by his path in two hours. In going up I went leisurely, stopping to sketch, and made a very good course until I got to the firs; but in coming down I missed my way, and probably travelled over four times as much ground as was necessary. It was from carelessness or indifference at the start—I was willing to make a day of it.

The view from under the cloud was very beautiful. The general character of the scenery is less grand than that of the White Mountains, but it has impressive sublimity and repose. All the mountains are covered with trees, which, with the luxuriant herbage beneath them, secures softness of outline. Brooks of clear water are frequent. The mountain sides are often very steep, but actual precipices or even large ledges or masses of rock, I have not seen. These mountains would therefore be more pleasant to ramble over than the White Mountains, and will probably, when railroads are completed in their neighborhood, be much resorted to for pleasure. At present there is no public

conveyance to any point within thirty-five miles of the base of "Balsam Mountain."

Mr. Buckley, a New York botanist, gives the following facts with regard to the mountains of this vicinity :

"The following are the heights of some mountains, and places among the mountains of North Carolina, south and west of Ashville. These heights were ascertained by me with two of Green's standard barometers. Professor J. Le Conte, of Columbia, South Carolina, observed the stationary barometer at Waynesville, for the measurement of the highest Smoky mountains, and being called away by the duties of his professorship, Miss S. Cathey, with the same barometer, made observations at the Forks of Pigeon, Haywood county, while I was with another barometer on the tops of the other mountains measured. The highest are in the Great Smoky or Unaka range of mountains, on the line between the States of North Carolina and Tennessee, near the head waters of the Oconaluftee and Little Pigeon rivers. You will observe that there are twelve peaks higher than Mount Washington, and two higher than Mount Mitchell, 6711 feet high, which has long been considered the highest East of the Rocky Mountains, viz. : Mount Le Conte, 6670; Mount Guyot, 6734; Mount Buckley, 6755; Clingman's Peak, 6941.

"Those high mountains show us why western North Carolina and eastern Tennessee have a northern climate in a southern latitude.

"These late measurements show us that the highest mountains at the South are not at the sources

of the largest rivers, as has generally been supposed.

"The highest mountains are covered with *Abies nigra* and *Abies Fraseri*, which are rarely found growing beneath an elevation of four thousand feet—the first being called by the inhabitants the he-balsam, and the latter the she-balsam. The *Abies balsamica* is not found there as stated by Michaux. A large moss (*Hypnum splendens*), often dotted with *Oxalis acetosella* and *Mitchella repens*, almost invariably forms a thick, soft carpet beneath these balsam trees. Our little red squirrel (*Sciurus Hudsonius*), there called the mountain buma, sports and chatters among these balsam trees, feeding on their cones. He rarely descends to the base of the mountains."

July 13.—I rode late last night, there being no cabins for several miles in which I was willing to spend the night, until I came to one of larger size than usual, with a gallery on the side toward the road and a good stable opposite it. A man on the gallery was about to answer (as I judged from his countenance), "I reckon you can," to my inquiry if I could stay, when the cracked voice of a worryful woman screeched out from within, "We don't foller takin' in people."

"No, sir," said the man, "we don't foller it."

"How far shall I have to go?"

"There's another house a little better than three quarters of a mile further on."

To this house I proceeded—a cabin of one room and a loft, with a kitchen in a separate cabin. The owner said he never turned anybody away, and I was wel-

come. He did not say that he had no corn, until after supper, when I asked for it to feed my horse. The family were good-natured, intelligent people, but very ignorant. The man and his wife and the daughters slept below, the boys and I in the cock-loft. Supper and breakfast were eaten in the detached kitchen. Yet they were by no means poor people. The man told me that he had over a thousand acres of rich tillable land, besides a large extent of mountain range, the most of which latter he had bought from time to time as he was able, to prevent the settlement of squatters near his valley-land. "There were people who would be bad neighbors I knew," he said, "that would settle on most any kind of place, and everybody wants to keep such just as far away from them as they can." (When I took my bridle off, I hung it up by the stable door ; he took it down and said he 'd hang it in a safer place. " He 'd never had anything stolen from here, and he did n't mean to have—it was just as well not to put temptation before the people," and he took it into the house and put it under his bed.)

Besides this large tract of land here, he owned another tract of two hundred acres with a house upon it, rented for one third the produce, and another smaller farm, similarly rented ; he also owned a gristmill, which he rented to a miller for half the tolls. He had also a considerable stock of cattle and large crops of grain, so that he must be considered a very respectable capitalist for a mountaineer. He told me that he had thought a good deal formerly of moving to new coun-

tries, but he had been doing pretty well and he had staid here now so long, he did n't much think he should ever budge. He reckoned he 'd got enough to make him a living for the rest of his life, and he did n't know any use a man had for more 'n that.

I did not see a single book in the house, nor do I think that any of the family could read. He said that many people here were talking about Iowa and Indiana; "was Hiaway (Iowa) beyond the Texies?" I opened my map to show him where it was, but he said he "was n't scollar'd enough" to understand it, and I could not induce him to look at it. I asked him if the people here preferred Iowa and Indiana to Missouri at all because they were Free States. "I reckon," be replied, "they don't have no allusion to that. Slavery is a great cuss, though, I think, the greatest there is in these United States. There ain't no account of slaves up here in the west, but down in the east part of this State about Fayetteville, there 's as many as there is in South Carolina. That 's the reason, the West and the East don't agree in this State; people out here hates the Eastern people."

"Why is that?"

"Why you see they vote on the slave basis, and there 's some of them nigger counties where there ain't more 'n four or five hundred white folks, that has just as much power in the Legislature as any of our mountain counties where there 'll be some thousand voters."

He made further remarks against slavery and against slave-holders. When I told him that I entirely agreed

with him, and said further that poor white people were usually far better off in the Free States than in the Slave, he seemed a little surprised and said, " New York ain't a Free State, is it?"

Laborer's wages here, he stated, were from fifty cents to one dollar a day, or eight dollars a month. " How much by the year?" " They's never hired by the year."

" Would it be $75 a year?"

" 'T wouldn't be over that, anyhow, but 't ain't general for people to hire here only for harvest time ; fact is, a man could n't earn his board, let alone his wages, for six months in the year."

" But what do these men who hire out during harvest time do during the rest of the year ; do they have to earn enough in those two or three months to live on for the other eight or nine?"

" Well they gets jobs sometimes, and they goes from one place to another."

" But in winter time, when you say there's not work enough to pay their board?"

" Well, they keeps a goin' round from one place to another, and gets their living somehow."

" The fact on 't is," he said at length, as I pressed the enquiry, " there ain't anybody that ever means to work any in this country, except just along in harvest —folks don't keep working here as they do in your country, I expect."

" But they must put in their crops?"

" Yes, folks that have farms of their own, they do

put in their craps and tend 'em, but these fellows that
don't have farms, they won't work except in harvest,
when they can get high wages [$8 a month]. I hired
a fellow last spring for six months; I wanted him to
help me plant and tend my corn. You see I had a
short crap last year, and this spring I had to pay fifty
cents a bushel for corn for bread, and I did n't want to
get caught so again, not this year, so I gin this fellow
$6 a month for six months—$36 I gin him in hard
silver.''

" Paid it to him in advance ? ''

" Yes, he would n't come 'less I 'd pay him right
then. Well, he worked one month, and maybe eight
days—no, I don't think it was more than six days over
a month, and then he went away, and I hain't seen a
sight on him since. I expect I shall lose my money—
reckon he don't ever intend to come back; he knows
I 'm right in harvest, and want him now, if ever I do.''

" What did he go away for ? ''

" Why he said he was sick, but if he was, he got well
mighty easy after he stopped working.''

" Do you know where he is now ? ''

" Oh, yes, he 's going round here.''

" What is he doing ? ''

" Well, he 's just goin' round.''

" Is he at work for any one else ? ''

" Reckon not—no, he 's just goin' round from one
place to another.''

At supper and breakfast surprise was expressed that
I declined coffee, and more still that I drank water in-

stead of milk. The women observed, "'t was cheap boarding me." The man said he must get home a couple more cows; they ought to drink milk more, coffee was so high now, and he believed milk would be just as healthy. The woman asked the price of coffee in New York; I could not tell her, but said I believed it was uncommonly high; the crops had been short. She asked how coffee grew. I told her as well as I was able, but concluded by saying I had never seen it growing. "Don't you raise coffee in New York?" she asked; "I thought that was where it came from."

The butter was excellent. I said so, and asked if they never made any for sale. The woman said she could make "as good butter as any ever was made in the yarth, but she could n't get anything for it; there war n't many of the merchants would buy it, and those that did, would only take it at eight cents a pound for goods." The man said the only thing he could ever sell for ready money was cattle. Drovers bought them for the New York market, and lately they were very high—four cents a pound. He had driven cattle all the way to Charleston himself to sell them, and only got four cents a pound there. He had sold corn here for twelve and a half cents a bushel.

Although the man could not read, he had honored letters by calling one of his children "Washington Irving;" another was known as Matterson (Madison?). He had never tried manuring land for crops, but said, "I do believe it is a good plan, and if I live I mean to try it sometime."

A COLONIZATIONIST

July 16*th*. I stopped last night at the pleasantest
house I have yet seen in the mountain ; a framed
house, painted white, with a log kitchen attached.
The owner was a man of superior standing. I judged
from the public documents and law books on his table
that he had either been in the Legislature of the State,
or that he was a justice of the peace. There were also
a good many other books and newspapers, chiefly of a
religious character. He used, however, some singularly
uncouth phrases common here. He had a store, and
carried on farming and stock-raising. After a conversation about his agriculture, I remarked that there
were but few slaves in that part of the country. He
wished that there were fewer. They were not profitable property here, I presumed. They were not, he
said, except to raise for sale ; but there were a good
many people here who would not have them if they
were profitable, and yet who were abundantly able to
buy them. They were horrid things, he thought ; he
would not take one to keep it if it should be given to
him. 'T would be a great deal better for the country,
he believed, if there were not a slave in it. He supposed it would not be right to take them away from
those who had acquired property in them without any
remuneration, but he wished they could all be sent out
of the country—sent to Liberia. That was what ought
to be done with them. I said it was evident that
where there were no slaves, other things being equal,
there was greater prosperity than where slavery sup-

plied the labor.   He did n't care so much for that, he
said ; there was a greater objection to slavery than
that, in his mind.   He was afraid that there was many
a man who had gone to the bad world who would n't
have gone there if he had n't had any slaves.   He had
been down in the nigger counties a good deal, and he
had seen how it worked on the white people.   It made
the rich people who owned the negroes, passionate and
proud and ugly, and it made the poor people mean.
" People that own niggers are always mad with them
about something ; half their time is spent in swearing
and yelling at them."

" I see you have *Uncle Tom's Cabin* here," said I ;
"have you read it ? "

" Oh, yes."

" And what do you think of it ? "

" Think of it ?   I think well of it."

" Do most of the people here in the mountains think
as you do about slavery ? "

" Well, there 's some thinks one way and some another, but there 's hardly any one here that don't think
slavery 's a curse to our country or who would n't be
glad to get rid of it."

I asked what the people about here thought of the
Nebraska Bill.   He couldn 't say what the majority
thought.   Would people moving from here to Nebraska
now, be likely to vote for the admission of slavery
there ?   He thought not ; most people would much
rather live in a Free State."   He told me that he knew
personally several persons who had gone to California

and taken slaves with them, who had not been able to bring them back. There were one or two cases where the negroes had been induced to return, and these instances had been made much of in the papers, as evidence that the slaves were contented.

"That's a great lie," he said; "they are not content, and nine tenths of 'em would do 'most any thing to be free. It's only now and then that slaves, who are treated unusual kind, and made a great deal of, will choose to remain in slavery if freedom is put in their way." He knew one man (giving his name), who tried to bring two slaves back from California, and had got started with them when some white people suspecting it, went on board the ship and told him it was against the law to hold negroes as slaves in California, and his negroes should n't go back with him unless they were willing to. Then they went to the slaves, and told them they need not return, if they preferred to stay, and the slaves said they had wanted very much to go back to North Carolina, yet they would rather remain in California, if they could be free, and so they took them ashore. He had heard the slaveowner himself relating this and cursing the men who interfered. He had told him that they did no more than Christians were obliged to do.

I overtook upon the road, to-day, three young men of the poorest class. Speaking of the price of land and the profit of farming, one of them said, believing me to be a Southerner: "We are all poor folks here; don't hardly make enough to keep us in liquor. Anybody

can raise as much corn and hogs on the mountains as he 'll want to live on, but there ain't no rich people here. Nobody 's got any black ones—only three or four ; no one 's got fifty or a hundred, like as they have down in the East." " It would be better," interrupted another, somewhat fiercely, " if there warn't any at all ; that 's my mind about it ; they 're no business here ; they ought to be in their own country and take care of themselves, that 's what I believe, and I don't care who hears it." But let the reader not be deceived by these expressions ; they indicate simply the weakness and cowardice of the class represented by these men. It is not slavery they detest ; it is simply the negro competition, and the monopoly of the opportunities to make money by negro owners, which they feel and but dimly comprehend.

HOW THEY TALK

A man said to me to-day, " It 's a heap warm."

The hail here, as in Texas, is " Travellin' ? " after which :

" Travelled a good piece ? " " What parts you been to ? " etc.

If you meet a man without stopping, the salutation always is, " How d' ye do, sir ? " never " Good morning "; and on parting it is, " I wish you well, sir," more frequently than " Good-bye." You are always commanded to appear at the table, as elsewhere throughout the South, in a rough, peremptory tone, as if your host feared you would try to excuse yourself.

"Come in to supper." "Take a seat. Some of the fry? Help yourself to anything you see that you can eat."

They ask your name, but do not often call you by it, but hail you "Stranger," or "Friend."

Texas is always spoken of in the plural—"the Texies." "Bean't the Texies powerful sickly?"

"Ill" is used for "vicious." "Is your horse ill?" "Not that I am aware of. Does he appear so?" "No; but some horses will bite a stranger, if he goes to handling on 'em."

"Is your horse ill?" "No, I believe not." "I see he kind o' drapt his ears when I came up, 'zif he was playful."

Everybody I've met in the last three counties—after ascertaining what parts I came from, and which parts I'm going to, where I got my horse, what he cost, and of what breed he is, what breed the dog is, and whether she's followed me all the way from the Texies, if her feet ain't worn out, and if I don't think I'll have to tote her if I go much further, and if I don't want to give her away, how I like the Texies, etc.—has asked me whether I didn't see a man by the name of Baker in the Texies, who was sheriff of —— county, and didn't behave exactly the gentleman, or another fellow by the name of ——, who ran away from the same county and cut to the Texies. I've been asked if they had done fighting yet in the Texies, referring to the war with Mexico.

HIGHWAYS AND BYWAYS

"The prosperity of a country can be best estimated from the character of its roads."—*Bushnell.*(?)

Elizabethton (pronounced Lizzi Bethton), *Tenn.*, *July* 15*th.*—You will be surprised to find me dating from Tennessee again. I have made a very crooked course. My only guide in planning out my route ahead has been *Mitchell's Traveller's Guide*. For the last month I have had my eye fixed upon a long stretch of straight road, running parallel to the North Carolina and Tennessee line, between Bakersville, N. C., and Greensville, Va. I was forced, after giving up the road by Knoxville, to go as far east as Ashville, North Carolina, whence, according to my map, there was a road by the French Broad to Bakersville. But I was advised that the regular road-route to Bakersville was further to the eastward, by Burnsville, so I fetched a course by Burnsville. Here, people disagreed about the road to Bakersville, and, as to Greensville, they had never heard of it. I found my way to Bakersville, however, the third day after leaving Ashville, by a difficult road—found, I should say, the guide-posts to Bakersville. Finally, reading "Bakersville, 1 M.," I rode the mile, but could see no town ; there were only three log cabins within a distance of a quarter of a mile. I asked a boy at the first of these, "How far is it to Bakersville?" "It's right up there." "How far?" "Oh, right up there." I passed the two other cabins, and just beyond them meeting two great Tennessee bacon wagons, I asked the driver of one how far

it was to Bakersville. He had never heard of the
place ; had seen no village in twenty miles. I rode
back to the last of the three cabins, but it was unoccupied, the door being fastened by a stake thrust into the
ground and pressed against it. I went to the next
cabin where I found an old man, of whom I asked,
" Is this house Bakersville ? "

" Yes, sir " (with gravity). He knew of no such
place as Greensville ; there was no road running hence
northwardly. There did use to be, he added, on second thought, a horsepath over the mountain to what
was called the " Fields of Tow," but it had n't been
used much for a long time, and he doubted if it could
be found now. Beyond the " Fields of Tow," he knew
of no track at all to the northward. The shortest way
into Virginia, he thought, was to cross the Iron mountain into Tennessee. My map (thus agreeing with his
advice), showed a road to Elizabethton, thence a
straight road to Greensville. So I followed the road
over the mountain, and soon found mile-posts reading
thus:

TOEBIOM.

(*i. e.*, To Eliza-Bethton, 10 miles). Here I find myself at fault again, there being no such road as is shown
in the map, to Greensville; at least, the post-master,
the inn-keeper, and two merchants of the place, know
of none. There is said to be a plain road, leading to
Abington in Virginia, which, as it is the only road to
the northward, I must, of course, follow.

SLAVE AND FREE IN THE HOUSEHOLD.

Northeastern Tennessee,——.—Night before last I spent at the residence of a man who had six slaves; last night at the home of a farmer without slaves. Both houses were of the best class common in this region; two-story framed buildings, large, and with many beds, to accommodate drovers and wagoners, who, at some seasons, fill the houses which are known to be prepared with stabling, corn, and beds for them. The slaveholder was much the wealthier of the two, and his house originally was the finer, but he lived in much less comfort than the other. His house was in great need of repair, and was much disordered; it was dirty, and the bed given me to sleep in was disgusting. He and his wife made the signs of pious people, but were very morose or sadly silent, when not scolding and re-ordering their servants. Their son, a boy of twelve, was alternately crying and bullying his mother all the evening till bed-time, because his father had refused to give him something that he wanted. He slept in the same room with me, but did not come to bed until after I had once been asleep, and then he brought another boy to sleep with him. He left the candle burning on the floor, and when, in five minutes after he had got into bed, a girl came after it, he cursed her with a shocking volubility of filthy black-guardism, demanding why she had not come sooner. She replied gently and entreatingly, "I did n't think you 'd have more 'n got into bed yet, Master John." The boys were talking and whispering obscenity till I

fell asleep again. The white women of the house were very negligent and sluttish in their attire ; the food at the table badly cooked, and badly served by negroes.

The house of the farmer without slaves, though not in good repair, was much neater, and everything within was well-ordered and unusually comfortable. The women and girls were clean and neatly dressed ; every one was cheerful and kind. There was no servant. The table was abundantly supplied with the most wholesome food—I might almost say the first wholesome food —I have had set before me since I was at the hotel at Natchez—loaf bread for the first time, chickens, stewed instead of fried, potatoes without fat, two sorts of simple preserved fruit, and whortleberry and blackberry pies. (The first time I have had any of these articles at a private house since I was in Western Texas.) All the work, both within and without the house, was carried on regularly and easily, and it was well done, because done by parties interested in the result, not by servants interested only to escape reproof or punishment.

Doubtless two extreme cases were thus brought together, but similar, if less striking, contrasts are found the general rule, according to my experience. It is a common saying with the drovers and wagoners of this country, that if you wish to be well taken care of, you must not stop at houses where they have slaves.

THE METHODISTS OF THE NORTHERN SOUTH

The man of the last described house was intelligent and an ardent Methodist. The room in which I slept

was papered with the *Christian Advocate and Journal,*
the paper of New York.[1] At the slaveholder's house,
my bedroom was partially papered with "Lottery
Schemes."

The free laboring farmer remarked, that, although
there were few slaves in this part of the country, he had
often said to his wife that he would rather be living
where there were none. He thought slavery wrong in
itself, and deplorable in its effects upon the white people.
Of all the Methodists whom he knew in northeastern
Tennessee and southwestern Virginia, he believed
that fully three fourths would be glad to join the
Methodist Church North if it were "convenient."
They generally thought slavery wrong, and believed
it the duty of the Church to favor measures to bring it
to an end. He was not an Abolitionist, he said ; he
did n't think slaves could be set free at once, but they
ought to be sent back to their own country, and while
they were here they ought to be educated. He had
perceived that great injustice was done by the people
both of the North and South towards each other. At

---

[1] RELIGION IN VIRGINIA.—A mass meeting of citizens of
Taylor County, Virginia, was held at Boothesville recently,
at which the following, among other resolutions, was passed
unanimously :

" That the five *Christian Advocates,* published in the cities
of New York, Pittsburg, Cincinnati, St. Louis, and Chicago,
having become Abolition sheets of the rankest character, we
ask our commonwealth's attorneys and post-masters to examine
them, and, if found to be of an unlawful character, to deal with
them and their agents as the laws of our State direct.— *Washington Republic.*

the South people were very apt to believe that the
Northerners were wanting not only to deprive them
of their property, but also to incite the slaves to bar-
barity and murder. At the North people thought that
the negroes were all very inhumanely treated. That
was not the case, at least, hereabouts it was n't. If I
would go with him to a camp meeting here, or to one of
the common Sunday meetings, I would see that the negroes were generally better dressed than the whites. He
believed that they were always well fed, and they were
not punished severely. They did not work hard, not
nearly as hard as many of the white folks; they were fat
and cheerful. I said that I had perceived this, and it
was so generally, to a great degree, throughout the
country; yet I was sure that on the large plantations
it was necessary to treat the slaves with great severity.
He "expected" it was so, for he had heard people
say, who had been on the great rice and cotton plantations in South Carolina that the negroes were treated
very hard, and he knew there was a man down here on
the railroad, a contractor, who had some sixty hands
which he had hired in Old Virginny ("that's what we
call eastern Virginia here"), and everybody who saw
them at work said he drove them till they could hardly
stand, and did not give them half what they ought to
have to eat. He was opposed to the Nebraska Bill, he
said, and to any further extension of slavery, on any
pretext; the North would not do its Christian duty if
it allowed slavery to be extended; he wished that it
could be abolished in Tennessee. He thought that

many of the people who went hence to Kansas would vote to exclude slavery, but he wasn't sure that they would do it generally, because they would consider themselves Southerners, and would not like to go against other Southerners. A large part of the emigration from this part of the country went to Indiana, Illinois, and Iowa, those States being preferred to Missouri because they were Free States. There were fewer slaves hereabouts now than there were when he was a boy. The people all thought slavery wrong except, he supposed, some slaveholders who, because they had property in slaves, would try to make out to themselves that it was right. He knew one rich man who had owned a great many slaves. He thought slavery was wrong, and he had a family of boys growing up, and he knew they would n't be good for anything as long as he brought them up with slaves; so he had told his slaves that if they wanted to be free he would free them, send them to Liberia, and give them a hundred dollars to start with, and they had all accepted the offer. He himself never owned a slave, and never would own one for his own benefit, if it were given to him, "first, because it was wrong, and secondly, because he did n't think they ever did a man much good."

I noticed that the neighbors of this man on each side owned slaves, and that their houses and establishments were much poorer than his.

SOUTHWESTERN VIRGINIA.

Abington, Va, July 17th.—Abington is a compact

little town, with a good deal of wealth. The country all about here, this side of the Virginia line, is rich and beautiful. The surface is rolling, with fine oak woods, clear of undergrowth, good pastures, luxuriant corn, and tolerable grain crops, good clover and grass. Land of the best, within three miles of the town, is worth $100; ten miles out, $25 an acre. The Virginia and Tennessee railroad is being constructed through this place. The hotel seems to be pretty well kept; everything is tolerable except the beds. While I was washing myself from head to foot a white man suddenly opened the door and looked at me for a minute in silence till I faced him.

"What yer doin'?"

"What am I doing?"

"Yes, what yer doin'?" (laughing.)

"Why, sir, can't you see?"

"Washin' on yer, he! he!"

"Yes."

"Yes, humph!" and he withdrew, laughing foolishly.

July 18*th*.—Left Abington. The country continues beautiful, rich, and productive, much like central New York. There are more slaves here than I have seen before for several weeks. Negroes and whites seem to be about equally employed in agricultural labor. I saw this morning about seven cradlers together. The leader was a negro, the second man a white, then four negroes, and a white at the foot. They were followed, as long as I could see them, by the owner

or overseer, who walked close behind them with a stick in his hand. An old man whom I overtook riding upon the road, told me that niggers had all been hired to work on the railroad at two hundred dollars a year. White laborers were paid ten dollars a month. "But," said he, "they don't do so much work here as they do in the north country. They say nobody works so hard here as they do where you come from ; neither niggers nor white men will do more than half as much in a day, so they say."

I passed upon the road two large flocks of sheep. The drivers said they had brought them from Western Tennessee, where they cost one dollar a head on an average. They intended to drive them two hundred miles further, into "the valley of Virginia," where they would be sold to farmers who would fatten them on meal, and sell them to drovers for the New York markets. They expect to get two dollars to three dollars a head. This sort of business is fast increasing in Virginia ; fatting cattle being found in most localities much more profitable than grain growing.

Agriculture in all Northern Virginia is, I apprehend, in a transition state, from pure grain to what English writers call "convertible husbandry," and the change is likely to progress, and, I think, will be unfavorable to slavery.

I stopped for the night at a large, handsome house ; the owner, a well-informed, thoughtful gentleman was evidently an excellent manager and master. In contrast with what I have recently seen, the house was

extremely clean and well-ordered, as were also the
gardens, stables, and other surroundings; the servants
were attentive, and I heard but one reproof of them
while I was in the house. The table was neat, the
food wholesome and well-cooked. I compared notes
with the gentleman upon crops and farm economy.
He said the average crop of the country was not over
eight bushels of wheat to the acre; his own crop last
year was twenty-seven (on a farm of four hundred acres
tillage land). The difference was principally owing to
more careful cultivation. He ploughed ten inches deep,
three horses to a plough. His usual crop of corn was
forty to fifty bushels to the acre, sometimes much
more.

He asked if I did not think as he did, that their climate here was more favorable to profitable agriculture
than that of New York. I thought that it was so for
all purposes of agriculture, except for the small grains.
"But," rejoined he, "you have one great advantage
over us. If I could get good laborers as easily as you
can in New York, I would never have another negro
on my place; it's a part of the evil we suffer from
slavery that it spoils our white men. Our white hands
are not, in general, a bit better than the negroes." He
employed several white hands and paid them ten dollars a month; and they wanted the same whether they
were hired by the year or only for the summer. They
did n't care to work for any great length of time without a change. They were very stupid at work, almost
as much so as the negroes, and could not be set to do

anything that required the least exercise of judgment,
unless he stood over them constantly. Yet he believed
that the white men, whom he had this year at $120 a
year wages, were worth more to him than the negroes
who were hired for $140. One of the latter was almost
useless, and this entirely from laziness and stupid indifference, for he was strong enough; he hardly paid
for his bread. Still there was that much that was inconvenient and unpleasant in employing white men,
especially where they were employed with negroes.

His white hands all were seated with us at the breakfast table; coarse, dirty, silent, embarrassed, and em-
barrassing men.

He afterwards observed that if they could get rid of
slaves, and obtain a sufficient number of white laborers
to do their field work, they would still have to employ
negro girls for the kitchen and household labor. The
white girls who would go out to work were worse than
the men, much worse than the negroes. He did not
know a white girl who would hire out, whose habits
were such that he could endure to have her in his
house. In fact, no girl hereabouts, whose character
was good, would ever hire out to do menial service.
There were some Maine gentlemen whom he knew,
who were professors in Emery and Henry College.
They thought slavery wrong, and they wouldn't buy
slaves, and had tried to get along with white girls,
but they were obliged to give it up, and pay owners
for the use of their slaves, as cooks and maids.

Abolition of slavery he thought impracticable. The

slaves could not take care of themselves. If they were freed and allowed to remain here, they would ruin the country. Every one knew, he said, that the State would be far more prosperous if the slaves were out of it. No doubt the State would be richer if they were all taken out of it without being paid for. He wished they might be.

July 19*th*.—Last night I spent with the family of a farmer who owned three or four negroes, and lived in a superior sort of log cabin quite comfortably. Indeed, a higher degree of comfort is generally evident since I entered Virginia. Although they had slaves, and there was a daughter, eighteen or twenty years old, I observed that they had a slovenly and very ugly white girl (possibly a very light mulatto), who seemed to be a servant, and who did not come to the table with the family, but gave the negroes their breakfast in the kitchen while we ate in an adjoining room with the door between the rooms open.

On a small table in the parlor were some books: the *Revival Miscellanies*, and the *Alarm to the Unconverted*, two Methodist Hymn Books, a large Bible, and a North Carolina Almanac, of the year before. The mother of the family, a very kindly fat old lady, officiated at family prayers.

"What yer done with yer gun?" inquired the mother; "see you've got your shot pouch."

"No, madam, it is not shot I carry in this pouch."

"No.—'Lowed 't wan't shot."

Silence and universal gravity, the eyes of the whole

family bent on my leather pocket for the next five
minutes. At length, a young man asks if I got much
gold in Texas. He had heard say there was powerful
good mines there. I told him there were no gold mines
in operation in Texas ; perhaps it was California he
meant. He did n't know but it was ; it was either
Texas or California ; he was sure he 'd heard people
say there was heaps of gold got out there.

These people told me that they had heard that some
Yankees (" that 's what they called people who came
from that part of the country," they parenthesized—
New Jersey Yankees,) had come down into Virginia
somewhere to raise stuff for New York. " They come
here because it is so much hotter, and they can raise
things earlier than they can about New York, and then
they take 'em on to New York. The New Yorkers is
so fond of novels that they 'll pay high for 'em to come
a little earlier."

July 20th.—After two farmers had declined to receive me, because, as they said, they had not got any
corn and were not prepared for travellers, and did not
like to take them in unless they could treat them well,
I stopped, near nine o'clock, at a house to which they
had recommended me, as the best within some miles.
It was a boarded log house, of four rooms and a gallery.
The owner was a farmer, with two hired white hands
besides his sons ; the whole family coarse, ignorant
people. As I took a seat for my supper, the mother
placed herself opposite to me, resting her two red scabby
arms on the table, smoking a pipe, and in the most

good-natured way, inquired into all the particulars of
my life as far as possible; whether I were married or not,
what "persuasion" (religious sect) my father and
mother belonged to, etc. etc. She had had some notion
of moving to Texas. A woman who went out from here
and settled there, wrote home that she had n't got any
cows of her own yet, but she could have the milking
of twenty, if she wanted, that belonged to the planters
around ; and she made butter and sold it at 37½ cents
a pound to the very men who owned the cows.
They were too lazy to make butter for themselves, but
they liked it so well they would pay 37½ cents a pound
for it. The old woman thought if she could get 37½
cents a pound for making butter, it would n't take long
for her to get rich, and "I 'd like to be rich," said she,
"not so rich as Wade Hampton, but so rich I need n't
do any more work." There had been several others
from hereabout, however, who went out to Texas and
did n't like it. There were two young men came back
last spring. They said 't was a right level flat country,
and 't was all of such deep, sticky mud, that it took five
pair of mules to haul a load of corn, and it was dreadful
sickly there, and there was n't any water at all ; all
that people had to drink was rain water that they caught
and kept. There men had, it appeared, landed at Gal-
veston or Indianola, gone back only a few miles from
the coast, lived there through a summer, and then returned disgusted with Texas, as well they might be if
that were all of it.

Although there were four rooms in the house, six of

us including a girl of fifteen, were bedded in one tight room.   There were no sheets at all on my bed, and what with the irritation of the feathers and the blanket, the impurity of the air, and a crying child, I did not fall asleep till near daylight.

Notwithstanding it was the middle of the harvest season, and they had mentioned to me that their oats had been struck with rust, and would lose value very rapidly every additional hour they remained uncut, there seemed to be no hurry about getting to work in the morning.   I hastened them all I could, in order to ride while the day was tolerably cool, but the sun was three hours high before breakfast was ready, and even when I rode away after it was finished, all the men and boys were lounging on the gallery, waiting to see me start, before they went afield ; nothing at all out of doors having been done before breakfast, not even the grinding of scythes.

The following day I descended the eastern slope of the Blue Ridge and came to that part of Virginia which was considered in the first volume of this work.[1]

Richmond, where I arrived a week later, somewhat surprised me by its substance, show, and gardens, and I was inclined to think that in coming to it directly from New York and Philadelphia, I had been led to rather underrate its quality at my first visit.[2]   There are only six towns, having a town-like character, in the Slave States—New Orleans, Mobile, Louisville, St. Louis,

[1] *Seaboard Slave States.*   [2] *Ibid.*

Charleston, and Richmond. Savannah, and all the other
"places" having, like it, in winter, a population for a
town, are simply overgrown villages in appearance, and
in convenience; half the streets tolerably good pastures,
the other half intolerable cartroads; the best mansions,
clap-board, Americo-moresque cottages; the best gardens in a setting of picket fence; the public squares
mere camp grounds, with weedy walks and sedge-grass
lawns; the majority of the shops selling raisins, nail-
rods and nigger-cloth, from the same counter with silks,
and school books and "bitters." Richmond, by contrast, is a metropolis, having some substantial qualities,
having a history, and something prepared for a future
as well. Compared with Northern towns of the same
population, there is much that is quaint, provincial, and
excessively slovenly, especially in whatever connects
directly with the country, such as the marketing. It is
only the mills and warehouses, a few shops and a few
private residences and hotels, that show real enterprise
or real and permanent wealth.

The Crawford Washington Monument is much the
highest attainment of American plastic art, and would
be a glory to any town or country but it points to the
past. What a failure has there been in the promises of
the past!

That, at last, is what impresses one most in Richmond. It is a metropolis, and, of course, the tide of
modern life elsewhere reaches it, stirs it, and here and
there possesses it, but yet it is plainly the metropolis of
Virginia, of a people who have been dragged along in

the grand march of the rest of the world, but who have had, for a long time and yet have, a disposition within themselves only to step backward.

Revolting from the generous and noble theories of Jefferson the essential difficulty with Virginians of to-day is want of faith in the capacity of men individually, white and black. Wealth, knowledge, and morality, are practically regarded as the accidents of men, not as their earnings. Slavery, and the laziness and faithlessness of the poor whites, are deplored, especially throughout the West, but every one says, and every one feels, it is hopeless to contend with these evils. "Slavery makes our poor whites worthless laborers; even slaves are better. The country languishes for want of laborers. No one then must be allowed to think of our dispensing with slaves." They thus acknowledge the cause of the evil; but show that they have not a spark of faith in the capacity of their poor whites to improve, even on the removal of this cause. This is what they mean, when they say, "It is impossible to abolish slavery"; —it is imposssible to live without somebody can be made to work. In every neighborhood, I found hope to center in something to come from without. A railroad or canal, which the Governor had recommended the State to aid; a copper or coal mine, or salt works, which some New Yorkers were talking about establishing; a new college, which some religious body proposed to found. But, lately, in the extreme West, where slaves are no direct impediment, a new hope seems to have got a lodgment, and where, even on the

frontier, a newspaper cannot be prevented from giving utterance to it, in such a manner as is done in the following paragraph from the *Wheeling Intelligencer*, it is impossible that it shall not bring with it at least a negative faith. A faith that will not resist, if it may not encourage, an infusion of such elements of improvement, as will make the obstruction which slavery presents to wealth, more and more obvious to all, at the same time that the possibility of dispensing with it is demonstrated.

"The present great and pressing want of our State, like that of the United States, is cultivation and improvement, not enlargement or annexation, and the obvious and the only mode of a rapid growth of our State or city, is such a change of public policy as shall invite to our aid and coöperation our Caucasian cousins, the intelligent, moral, and industrious artisans, mechanics, miners, manufacturers, farmers, and commercial men of Europe and the Northern States, to share our taxation, develop our resources, and make ours a white man's country, with all the energy, education, love of order, of freedom, and of progress characteristic of the Anglo-Saxon race. The history of the world, and especially of the States of this Union, shows most conclusively that public prosperity bears an almost mathematical proportion to the degree of freedom enjoyed by all the inhabitants of the State. Men will always work better for the cash than for the lash. The free laborer will produce and save as much, and consume and waste as little as he can. The slave, on the contrary, will produce and save as little, and consume and waste as much as possible. Hence States and counties filled with the former class must necessarily flourish and increase in population, arts, manufactures, wealth, and education, because they are animated and incited by all the vigor of the will ; while States filled with the latter class must exhibit comparative stagnation, because it is the universal law of nature that force and fear end in ruin and decay."

CHAPTER VII

PATRIARCHAL LIFE IN VIRGINIA, AND IN GENERAL

JAMES RIVER CHAT

FROM Richmond I went with my horse and dog direct to New York by the steamer. There were but few first-class passengers; the majority of those who did not leave at the river landings, or at Norfolk, being Northern men, or men of Northern birth doing business at the South, and going North with their families for the remainder of the summer.

Of the project of a line of "mammoth steamships," to be established between Richmond and Antwerp, with the assistance of mail patronage from the United States, and loans from the Belgian and Virginian governments, which, when I was last on James River, was the exciting topic of conversation, I now no longer heard a word spoken. The party of progress, however, represented by six gentlemen in black, with gold-headed walking-sticks, sitting in caucus around a spittoon by the side of the wheel-house, as we were carefully floated in ballast over the shoals, were equally animated in the confidence of some new scheme, which it was deemed equally safe and respectable to discuss publicly, and which it was held with equal confidence would be the sure salvation of old Virginia.

38

My room-mate proved to be a Mississippian, lazy and amiable, a sort of smouldering fire-eater. He sneered at the Virginians and their speculations, and held men to be little better than fools who would keep niggers to make corn and tobacco, when by moving them to his own region, and setting them to make cotton, they might easily double their incomes. But they did not keep them to make corn, he said, they kept them to breed and raise young ones. It was folly to pretend that they did not. A man might not raise a nigger with a well-considered plan to sell him eighteen years after he was born; he might never sell a nigger, but for all that, it was the readiness with which he could command a thousand dollars for every likely boy he had, if he should ever need it, that made him stay here and be bothered with taking care of a gang of niggers who barely earned enough to enable his family to live decently. He did not sell them, because he thought they were a good investment to hold, and men were proud of being able to hold a big lot of niggers. There were not many men here, either, who did not sell their niggers off, some of them, every year or two; whenever they wanted money. Some pretended that they only sold the rascals, but the rascals they sold were generally likely boys, just the thing for cotton pickers, and would bring more money than the slow men and the women whom they kept. If they did not sell them off, why were not the stocks larger? There were a few men here who owned a hundred or two niggers, but not nearly as many as in Mississippi, and yet every-

body knew a nigger stock would naturally increase twice as fast here as it would in Mississippi. What became of them if they were not sold ? He had never sold a nigger in his life, but he had bought a good many, and two thirds of them were fresh from Virginia. He had one boy who said that the man who raised him had sold him to get the money to pay for a piano which he had bought for his daughter. A gentleman would never think of doing such a thing as that in Mississippi. He would always calculate to pay from his crop.

I have more than once observed that the rich men of the Southwest feel themselves rather a superior class to the Virginians, somewhat as the rich Virginia country-gentlemen look upon Northern farmers—as if agriculture in a free-labor country were necessarily a small and rather mean business. The following passage from an article in the Brandon *Republican*, a Mississippi newspaper, manifests the general incredulity with regard to the assertion that slaves are not bred for commercial purposes in Virginia and the adjoining States, which it is impossible to resist in regions where half the population of a county often consists of negroes who have been sold from that State :

" Now let us consider the probable consequences of drawing upon the savage and barbarous hordes of Africa for slaves to compete with our own, and most likely eventually drive out of Southern markets the slave breeders of the South. Are there not, including South Carolina—although for the last eight or ten years she has thrown upon us more slaves than any one of the old Slave States—six States that must hereafter derive

profit from breeding slaves for the Southern States or derive no profit from the institution? We mean Delaware, Maryland, Virginia, North Carolina, Kentucky, and Missouri. Nearly one third of the population of these States are slaves. If slave labor cannot be made to pay there—and we hear it continually asserted that this labor can not be advantageously employed in grain-growing countries—then what are they to do with their slaves if this policy is inaugurated and they are excluded from Southern markets, they being forced to retain in their hands property which can make no adequate return for the expenses of feeding, clothing, etc.? Do you think, reader, that any surer means could be employed to call into existence an abolition sentiment there than that of forcing these States to retain in their territory a large and expensive body of slaves that they can not find remunerative employment for? No practical man will believe that they will keep them when the time comes that they can not be turned to profit. Should they be shut out from the Southern markets, with their heavy slave population to 'harass them and eat out their substance,' and almost unproductive and rapidly producing, how can they keep them? Let it come to this, and we predict that their owners will get rid of them, even if they are compelled to incur the expenses of their shipment to Africa. Allow them still to find a profit in slave breeding, and their affection for the institution will remain as fixed as 'Ixion on his wheel.' "

To the same effect is the following admission of the Charleston *Standard* in an article on agricultural improvement at the South:

"The Virginia journalists have repeatedly borne witness to the fact, that in many districts, where large estates have been divided and sold to small farmers, the land is turning off from three to six times as much produce as it did a few years ago. [1] "

This is much the same as saying, that from certain limited districts of Virginia, where slavery has been practically abandoned (the slaves having been sold off by the sheriff in most cases) the contribution of the

[1] Charleston *Standard*, August 17, 1854.

earth to the comfort of the human race has almost immediately been increased fourfold.

Once again, during the afternoon, I had the pleasure of witnessing a scene similar to those described in the first volume,[1] in the same locality, the joyful welcome of white people, returning to their plantation, by their house-servants; and again I noticed the comparative indifference of the field-hands or common slaves, who barely touched their tattered hats and grinned, before lifting on to each other's heads the trunks which were to be thus carried to the house after the carriage which bore the whites and upper servants altogether. This humbler kind did not say one word to their master or mistress, and only grinned in sympathy with the excitement of the young people, nor were they spoken to at all, so far as I observed.

I am here reminded that I may seem to have hitherto too much overlooked a certain view of Southern life, much delighted in by novelists and poets, and not usually neglected by travellers. I mean that which, in debates, is commonly alluded to when the terms "patriarchal," "paternal," "filial," "tutelary," and "pupilage," are used, the two latter terms being less frequently heard of late years than in the early days of the republic.

The truth is, that I have made, as all travellers are inclined to make, the most I honestly could of every instance or indication of such a relation as these terms express, that I have seen. Anything of the kind is always interesting, and gratifying to read of and to write

[1] *Seaboard Slave States.*

of, as it is to witness. Would I then have it inferrred that Slavery has been too much honored in this respect? I must say that such is my conviction.

Will the reader consider how many poets and novelists, and what is of more consequence, how many apparently matter-of-fact travellers speak of our Yankee tars otherwise than as gallant, jolly, and generous fellows, or of the red Indian otherwise than as the calm, sad, dignified child of nature—" the noble savage." And yet the reader probably knows, if he has taken the trouble to look the facts in the face, regardless of traditions and predispositions, that American seamen (seagoing) as a class, are more wretched, and are governed more by threats of force than any other civilized laborers of the world. There are exceptions. There are ports from which when ships are manned the rule is otherwise. But at our great ports, New York, Philadelphia, Baltimore, the sailor of sea-going ships, nine times out of ten, when sober and not led to do otherwise by vanity or a desire to satisfy your romantic interest, will tell you that he hates the sight of blue water, that he habitually hates his ship, hates his officers, hates his messmates, and despises himself. And as for the red man of nature, when found in a state of nature, what, in fact, is he? Nine times out of ten experience will say that the description which in the second volume of this work[1] I quoted, as best expressing my own observation among the most natural and the most warlike, that is, the most murderous and every way

[1] *Journey in Texas.*

detestable tribes on the continent, is no libel ; — "a conceited, tiresome, bloodthirsty, monotonous humbug."

Civilization is, in fact, the best condition of mankind, and ,the steps by which mankind have arrived at civilization do not need to be retraced to find morality, respectability, or happiness.

The supposition of a master's occupying the position of a father toward his slaves and of the slaves accepting this relation, affectionately, faithfully, and confidingly, is an improbable one. Imagine a household consisting of first a man and wife, second an ordinary family of sons and daughters, for whom the parents must have a special affection, and who must be favored and petted, as compared with—third, twenty to fifty additional sons and daughters, of all ages, the majority being adults, however, but all subject in all their movements, not to the influence and advice merely, but absolutely and abjectly, to the will, of their parents, not being able to eat or drink, or to dress, or to engage in any business, or to pursue any inclination of taste, or to marry, except with the approval of their father, not even after marriage to be any more independent than before. There is not one man among millions whose household under such circumstances would not be a pandemonium. The slaves are not their master's children ; he is not affected in his government of them by the instinctive regard for their happiness which a parent might have.

The patriarchal condition of society is, in fact, an

exceedingly rude, uncomfortable, and low state of society, only endurable by indolent, wandering men, who are obliged for purposes of defense to remain attached, on any terms which may be required, to the most convenient nucleus of combined strength which is offered them. If a solitary wanderer on the great plains without arms or food should be overtaken by a family of wanderers, and the father should offer to supply him with food, and to furnish him with means of defense, on condition that he would obey his orders and attach his fortunes to those of the family, he would probably accept the proposal, and would remain in irksome dependence so long as the family were subject to the dangers of the wilderness, but as soon as the opportunity of fixed settlements and a peaceable organization of many independent families made it possible, he would form other and various associations, and direct his movements according to his own judgment, for his own good, and it would doubtless be for the best good of all concerned that he should do so.

The patriarchal condition is a transitional one. If long maintained it must be by an abuse of intelligence and at the expense of comfort and morality. It then ceases to be paternal and becomes oppressive; becomes degrading, both in patriarch and patriarchate. The true teaching of history is clearly expressed in the following passage from Mill's *Political Economy* : [1]

"The theory of dependence and protection is an idealization, grounded on the character and conduct of here and there

[1] *Principles of Political Economy*, ii., 325.

an individual.   All privileged and powerful classes, as such, have used their power in the interest of their own selfishness, and have used their self-importance in despising and not in lovingly caring for those who were, in their estimation, degraded, by being under the necessity of working for their benefit.   I do not affirm that what has always been always must be, or that human improvement has no tendency to correct the intensely selfish feelings engendered by power ; but though the evil may be lessened, it cannot be eradicated until the power itself is withdrawn.   This, at least, seems to me undeniable, that long before the superior classes could be sufficiently improved to govern in the tutelary manner supposed, the inferior classes would be too much improved to be governed."

 This, written with no reference to Slavery, is my experience, the lesson taught at all points by Slavery, to-day, in our nation.

CHAPTER VIII

SLAVERY EXTENSION; SOUTHERN COMMERCE AND
COTTON SUPPLY; PRESENT CONDITION AND CHAR-
ACTER OF THE CITIZENS OF THE SOUTH; THE
CAUSES AND THE REMEDY

To observe the condition and character of the citizens
was my principal object while travelling in the Slave
States; to contribute toward a study of the practical
workings of the system of which their condition and
character must be the truest exponent is the principal
object of these volumes. That system, while it rests
on slavery, is not simply slavery, but is slavery of the
peculiar kind which exists alone in our republic, including especially the various laws, habits, and political
and social customs which are designed to secure its in-
violability and perpetuity, and by which any modification, improvement, or different arrangement, is resisted.
American slavery is not merely a system for the subjection and government, under individual masters, of
a certain number of slaves. It is, for instance, a system
of colonization as well.

Most of the citizens of the Slave States appear to
believe that the continuance of slavery depends upon

the continual and rapid territorial dispersion of the slave-holding community. Whether they are right or not, such a movement is at present a distinguishing and essential fact of American slavery. If an American slave-holding community could be other than a very loosely organized community, American slavery would be, in that community, a different thing from what it is now everywhere found to be. In Virginia itself, an essentially frontier condition of society prevails to this day. Beasts and birds of prey, forests, and marshes are increasing; bridges, schools, churches, and shops diminishing in number, where slavery has existed longest. The habits of the people correspond.

There are various other circumstances at present peculiar and essential to the system of American slavery, which might be changed, and yet slavery remain, but such slavery would not be the system which is now discussed, nor would its effects be the same. When speaking of the slavery of our Slave States, then, I mean not slavery simply, but all those habits, customs, and laws, which at present invariably accompany, and are peculiarly connected with the slave system as it at present exists in our own country.

The Slave States are vast territorially. There are, independent of slavery, important circumstances acting in their different parts, hence a study of the condition of the people must be an extended and tedious one, nor can facts or phenomena in sufficient number to enable the reader to form an estimate for himself, of the effects which it is right to ascribe simply to slavery

and the customs, habits, and laws, which at present belong to the slave system, be given otherwise than in a long and circumstantial narrative.

In previous volumes,[1] the grand divisions of old settlement and of recent settlement, have been separately considered. In the present volume, my experience and observations with regard to two distinct divisions have been narrated. The first, a region which, independent of slavery, is unquestionably able to yield a larger money value for agricultural labor than any other in the world, it being the favored soil, in the favored climate, with the cheapest natural facilities of transportation to a market, of that production, for which there is the most urgent commercial demand; the second, widely different, being distant from markets, with no peculiar agricultural productions, and offering but small rewards for agricultural labor.

In the latter, the mountainous region, the people are poor, and there are but few slaves. It is true that nearly all have either themselves been educated in the slave-holding districts, or are the direct descendants, and but one or two generations removed, from persons so educated; but slavery at present exercises scarcely any direct effect upon them. Whether in consequence of this exemption or not, they differ noticeably in character, customs, and habits from the people of the slave-holding districts. Their own impression that the absence or scarcity of slaves is the cause of this difference, and that this is a matter of congratulation, was expressed to me every day while I was among

[1] *Seaboard Slave States* and *Journey in Texas.*

them, nor was any doubt of it even once intimated to
me. Compared with the slaveholders, these people
are more cheerful, more amiable, more sociable, and
more liberal. Compared with the non-slaveholders of
the slave-holding districts, they are also more hopeful,
more ambitious, more intelligent, more provident, and
more comfortable. Their general poverty can not be
thought to result from the absence of slaves. Rather
it is the small reward for labor which agriculture in
the mountains offers, and their consequent inability to
accumulate capital, which prevents them from possessing slaves. Such difference as is most obvious and
general between them and the people of the mountain
regions in the Free States may be confidently attributed
to their distance from markets (including markets of
intelligence) and the consequent want of variety in
their occupation.

The distinguishing element of the condition of the
other region considered in this volume, is the extraordinary value which attaches to labor within it, in consequence of the peculiar favorableness of the soil and
climate for the production of cotton.

It is quite plain, notwithstanding all the drawbacks
attending the employment of forced labor, and notwithstanding the high price of slaves, that slave labor
is employed profitably by the large planters in Mississippi, and in certain other parts of the South, in the
culture of cotton. That the profit, in this case, is not
only large compared with the profit of slave labor
employed elsewhere, and in other occupations, but

that it is moderately good, at least, compared with the profit of other investments of capital and enterprise at the North and in Europe, must also be admitted. There are few enterprises to which capital lends itself more freely than to speculation in slaves, when the seeker for it is already a large cotton planter.

Is slave labor, then, profitable?

To certain individuals, unquestionably.

Nor do I think myself warranted in denying that the production of cotton per acre on many Mississippi plantations may not be as large as it can be economically made with land as low and slaves as high in price as is at present the case.

Is not then this slave agriculture economically conducted?

To the ends had in view by the planter it certainly is.

I answer thus distinctly, because assertions to the same effect have been addressed to me, evidently with the supposition that they invalidated the argument on the economy of Virginia, and of other parts of my first volume. That argument was intended to lead to the conclusions that the cost of such labor as is usually performed by slaves in Virginia, is more than double, in that State, what it is in New York. That in consequence of this excessive cost of labor, the profits of agriculture are much less than they would be if free trade in the commodity of labor could be established. That it is a consequence also of this high cost of labor that enterprise and capital avoid Virginia, especially avoid agriculture in Virginia, and that, as might there-

fore be supposed, agriculture in Virginia is a wretch-
edly conducted business, and among the agricultural
class, niggardness, surliness, and bigoted ignorance
much more prevail than among the farmers of the
Free States. In short, that slavery, by unnecessarily
adding to the cost of making natural wealth, or the
resources of the country, available, and by causing a
wasteful use of natural wealth, has the effect of impov-
erishing and degrading Virginia.

The difference between Virginia and Mississippi is
mainly found in the fact that in the latter State cotton
grows luxuriantly and matures perfectly. The demand for cotton is such, and the soil on which it
can be grown is so limited, that wherever it can be
produced with facility a given investment in land,
tools, and labor will be much better rewarded than
a similar investment can be rewarded in any agricultural enterprise in Virginia. What is true with
regard to Virginia, I believe to be true with regard to
Mississippi, with only this difference, that in Mississippi there is one description of natural wealth available with so little labor (having regard to its value in
the world) that even with the disadvantages of slavery, capital appears for a time to be well invested in
developing it, hence agriculture; that is to say, cotton
culture in Mississippi attracts capital, enterprise, and
skill, as corn culture would in Virginia if the value of
corn bore the same relation to the cost of the labor
employed in its production.

The cost of labor merely, is as much increased by

slavery in Mississippi as it is in Virginia; the cost of production, the barrier to wealth, is as much more than it needs to be in Mississippi as it is in Virginia. The necessary loss appears to me to be larger in Mississippi, indeed. Substitute a free trade of labor in Mississippi for the present system, and I suppose that you will have, as you would in Virginia, a fourfold value of land, a fourfold economy.

I repeat: Slave labor is to-day undoubtedly profitable to certain owners of slaves in Mississippi.

It was undoubtedly profitable to roll tobacco in casks one hundred miles to market, at one time, in Virginia.

It would probably be profitable in Illinois to reap wheat with sickles, and thrash it with flails, and market it by wagons, if there were no horse reaping machines and horse thrashing machines, and steam locomotive machines, engaged in supplying the demand for wheat, but there is many hundred-fold the wealth in Illinois to-day that there would have been had sickles, flails, and wagon trains been held to there with the same bigotry as is slavery in Mississippi; and if it could be made certain that ten years hence the present labor system of Mississippi would be superseded by the free labor system, I have little doubt that twenty years hence the wealth of Mississippi would be at least tenfold what, under the present system, it is likely to be, and the whole country and the whole world be some degrees happier than it is now likely to be.

But this is conjectural.   What is the actual condition of the people of Mississippi to-day ?

In Mississippi (and in the rich lowland cotton regions generally of the Slave States) the social phenomena are found most satisfactory in districts wherein a fixed community has for many years been established, and the fertility of the soil not yet largely exhausted. Evidences of wealth, of education, religion, and refinement will never be wanting among the citizens of such a district, nor evidences of a bantling civilization and of a certain degree of rude comfort among the other part of the people.   Among the citizens there may, indeed, be but very few indigent or uninstructed ; possibly on several square miles not one such family will be resident.   At no great distance, however, there may, I believe, invariably be found some tract of sterile or less fertile land, a large majority of the inhabitants of which are extremely poor and ignorant whites, stupidly contented, helpless and hopeless in their ignorance and poverty.

I have on my desk, as I write, and I write only after seeing how fully the judgment to which I am compelled from my own scrutiny of the ground is confirmed by it, evidence published by many partisans of the extension of slavery enough to half fill this volume, of which, to corroborate the sweeping assertion just made, I need give here but a single example :

"I am not aware that the relative number of these two classes has ever been ascertained in any of the States, but I am satisfied that the non-slaveholders far outnumber the slaveholders, per-

haps by three to one.[1]   In the more southern portion of this region ['the south-west,' of which Mississippi is the centre], the non-slaveholders possess generally but very small means, and the land which they possess is almost universally poor and so sterile that a scanty subsistence is all that can be derived from its cultivation, and the more fertile soil, being in the hands of the slaveholder, must ever remain out of the power of those who have none. * * * And I lament to say that I have observed of late years that an evident deterioration is taking place in this part of the population, the younger portion of it being less educated, less industrious, and, in every point of view, less respectable than their ancestors." [2]

And, for the present, I ask that what is said by this writer of the material condition of two thirds of the whole population of his own quarter, which, in its natural resources, is the very richest region at this moment in the known world, may be assumed to be true of the majority of the people of the South, as, I believe, no ingenuous Southern gentleman will deny that it is.

Is their condition the result of poverty caused merely by a poor return for labor which is yielded by such a soil?   I say that it is not, because I know that the occupants of similar soils at the North are far superior to them in nearly every quality, habit, and attainment which civilized men respect and value.   Is their condition the result of climate ?   The conviction in my mind that it is not, has been formed from innumerable personal observations and some personal experience.   The recent German settlers in Texas and in South Carolina, the whites on steamboats and railroads and in trade,

[1] It was not long since estimated in the Legislature of Kentucky as seven to one in that State.

[2] De Bow's *Resources of the South and West*, vol. ii., p. 106.

the white workmen in New Orleans, as well as thousands of exceptional, hardworking, and successful laboring Southerners testify that the climate is no preventive of persevering toil by the white race in any part of the Slave States. I have, in fact, seen more white native American women at work in the hottest sunshine in a single month, and that near midsummer, in Mississippi and Alabama than in all my life in the Free States, not on account of an emergency, as in harvesting, either, but in the regular cultivation of cotton and of corn, chiefly of cotton.

Further evidence leading to the same conclusion, I find in the fact that men born, nurtured, and trained in the South show no lack of strength or endurance when engaged in athletic exercise which is immediately gratifying to their ambition, passions, or their tastes. The climate prohibits no sort of labor, except such as would be generally productive of wealth, to the white man of the South.[1] How is this to be explained?

In part, at least, thus, is it not? (I ask, and I hope the reader will not neglect to answer according as he is well persuaded.) All mankind have an intuitive respect for strength or power. Slavery is the most palpable evidence of weakness or the involuntary subjection of strength in the slave. That is the meaning of slavery. The condition of a slave, therefore, as compared with that of a man independent of another's will, so far as

[1] See the evidence of Mr. Darby and others in *Seaboard Slave States*. See also *Texas Journey*. Additional testimony on this point from Southern experts may be found further on.

that condition of him is alone concerned, is universally regarded with the absence of respect, with something of contempt or pity. Whatever is associated with the slave as having been peculiarly attached to his condition is regarded with a certain degree of similar feeling. Manual agricultural labor is the chief employment of slaves in the South. For manual agricultural labor, therefore, the free man looking on, has a contempt, and for its necessity in himself, if such necessity exists, a pity quite beyond that of the man under whose observation it has been free from such an association of ideas.

Slaves are not wholly confined to agricultural labor, it is true, but it is equally true that in proportion as they are engaged in other employments are the whites who are also engaged in these employments found to be generally indolent, careless, untrustworthy, and unsuccessful. That such persons are conscious of the degradation which attaches to the employment of slaves is manifested in the fierce hostility of white mechanics to the instruction of slaves in their crafts, for this opposition is not at all relative or proportionate to the effect of such use of slaves in reducing their wages. It is not the mere competition of slaves in the market which throws white men out of it. If it were, labor contracts could be made at a lower rate in the Slave than in the adjoining Free States, whereas the contrary is the case.[1]

[1] Of course I do not refer to contracts for the *time* of laborers or workmen, which, owing to their indolence and unskilfulness, are frequently lower for whites at the South than at the North. So few Southerners hesitate to admit this effect of

"The poor white man," Mr. De Bow tells us, "will endure the evils of pinching poverty rather than engage in servile labor;"[1] and the white woman would, "however humble in the scale of society, consider such services a degree of degradation to which she could not condescend, and she has, therefore, no resource but to suffer the pangs of want and wretchedness." And J. H. Tyler, Esq., of Charleston, in defending an effort to employ whites in manufactories in South Carolina against the charge that it might tend to injure the value of slaves, says :

---

slavery, and it has been so forcibly set forth by Jefferson and most other statesmen of the South, that it may seem supererogatory to argue its existence or importance. I observe, however, that of late not a few Democratic journalists of the North have shown a disposition to discredit it, and nearly all to make light of it. A friend of Senator Douglas, for instance, said recently in the *Mattoon Gazette :*

"We are one of those that utterly discredit the idea that the presence of slaves works an injury to the whites. * * * We candidly and firmly believe to-day that if Illinois were a Slave State the best men of Kentucky, Virginia, Tennessee, and even States further South, would be here as soon as they could remove their families, and the prairies of Illinois would be made to smile as a lovely garden. We have seen the best class of men come to our State, admire it with enthusiasm, but return to their homes because they could not bring their whole families with them."

Judge Nichols, of Kentucky, whose opportunity of observation was probably better than this gentleman's, and whose character and position entitle his views to particular respect, said, in a speech, in 1837 : "The deliberate convictions of my most matured consideration are, that the institution of slavery is a most serious injury to the habits, manners, and morals of our white population ; that it leads to sloth, indolence, dissipation, and vice."

---

[1] *Resources of the South*, vol. i., p. 241.

" The poor man has a vote as well as the rich man, and in our State the number of the former will largely overbalance the latter. So long as these poor but industrious people could see no mode of living except by a degrading operation of work with the negro upon the plantation, they were content to endure life in its most discouraging forms, satisfied they were *above* the slave, though faring often worse than he."[1]

Many writers attempt, in my opinion, to attach an entirely undeserved "honor to labor." Mere plodding manual labor is not in itself honorable. Dexterity, ingenuity in the application of labor, industry, and perseverance are honorable traits in all men, but labor in itself is not honorable. On the other hand, in no enlightened free community is labor in itself practically degrading, because hireling labor is everywhere the stepping-stone from poverty and mediocrity to comfort and a position of usefulness. But in the South the step has become, if we are to believe Mr. De Bow (as quoted above,) a degradation which the poorest white considers more grievous than the " pangs of want and wretchedness."

It is sometimes said that this feeling of degradation only exists when the free laborer works in the same gang or the same field with slaves, or that at furthest it extends only to hired laborers working under the direction of their employers, that it does not lessen the industry of men working on their own account. The observation above quoted from Mr. De Bow may be intended to be so restricted. In view of notorious facts, of which many have been already cited in this

[1] De Bow's *Review*, January, 1850.

work from other and equally respectable advocates of
the slave social system, the reader may judge how far
this theory is philosophically probable. I will only
say here that I have seen nothing in the South to lead
me to entertain it.

Not that I have seen no industrious white men at
the South. I have seen many, and seen them side by
side with slaves. There are incentives to industry
acting counter to this influence of slavery, which in
certain situations can not fail to be in some degree
effective, for there is probably no country in the world
where nature offers a better reward for intelligent labor
than in some parts of the Slave States. When, indeed,
this is considered, the mere popular degradation of
labor arising from its association with the idea of subjection and submission to the will of a master, does not
seem adequate to account for the actual excessive indolence, folly, and poverty of the majority of the people
of the South. Nor does it, for that would be a result
of slavery simply, of any slavery. American slavery,
as at present advocated, American slavery, as it is
desired to be perpetuated, nourished, protected, and
extended, has an influence far more cruel, more strenuously repressive upon the mass of free citizens than
slavery elsewhere ever did; than slavery in itself at all
need to have; than, with all possible safety, with all
reasonable profitableness to the owners of slaves, it is
my judgment that it needs to have.

I hope that those who have read what I, as an eye-
witness have described, in this and the preceding

volumes,[1] will have acquired, if they did not otherwise
possess, some understanding of the manner in which
slavery, as it is now maintained in our Slave States,
operates very generally to put a limit, and a very short
limit, upon the natural motives which should impel a
free man to live industriously.   No theoretic explanation can be sufficient, if the facts, the abundant facts,
which no intelligent traveller who has really penetrated
the South has failed to acquire, which no sincere
patriot of the South attempts to disguise, are not
strongly impressed upon the mind of the investigator.

The accidental discovery of a palliative sometimes
indicates unerringly the true nature of a disease and
makes its remedy simple.   I think that I always felt
the poverty of the whites of the South, in the midst of
so much inert wealth, to be somewhat mysterious; I
had no such prejudice against American slavery that I
felt satisfied with it as the sole cause, until I caught
sight of a fragment of the annual report of the president
of a South Carolina manufacturing company.   This
presiding manufacturer is not a Massachusetts spinner,
nor a New York merchant, but a well-known and a
much and worthily respected citizen of Charleston,
William H. Gregg, Esq.   In his report, Mr. Gregg,
in a manner characteristic of his class and his education, withdraws the attention of his directors as soon
as practicable from the mere commercial view of their
enterprise, and shows its higher interest as a social
experiment.   I quote:

[1] *Seaboard Slave States* and *Journey in Texas.*

"The population of Graniteville is made up mainly from the poor of Edgefield, Barnwell, and Lexington districts."

Before going further, it is well that it should be known that the "poor" of these districts are by no means more destitute of educational and religious privileges than the poor men, on an average, within the planting regions. By reference to the census returns I find that they are provided with public schools at the rate of one to less than thirty square miles, while within the State of South Carolina, inclusive of its several towns, there is but one public school on an average, to every forty square miles. There are churches within these districts, one to about seventeen square miles; throughout the State, including Charleston and its other cities, one to every twenty-five square miles. In Georgia the average is one to thirty-two square miles. With the condition of the newer cotton States, in these respects, that of Edgefield, Barnwell, and Lexington would be found to compare still more favorably for the poor. In Lexington there is even a theological seminary. Nevertheless, even in these districts, there must have been not a little destitution and ignorance, for Mr. Gregg goes on congratulating the stockholders on what their enterprise has accomplished:

"From extreme poverty and want, they have become a thrifty, happy, and contented people. When they were first brought together, the *seventy-nine* out of a hundred grown girls who could neither read nor write were a by-word around the country; that reproach has long since been removed. We have night, Sunday, and week-day schools. Singing-masters, music-teachers, writing-masters, and itinerant lecturers all find pa-

tronage in Graniteville, where the people can easily earn all
the necessaries of life, and are in the enjoyment of the usual
luxuries of country life." * * *

"To get a steady supply of workmen, a population must be
collected *which will regard themselves as a community*, and
two essential elements are necessary to the building up, moral
growth, and stability of such a collection of people, namely, a
church and a schoolhouse." * * *

The truth of these views Mr. Gregg establishes by
the failure of manufacturing enterprises at the South in
which they have been disregarded.   From these fail-
ures the opinion has obtained that the poor whites
were not available as laborers, and that in all industrial
enterprises the capitalists would be obliged to employ
slave labor.   Mr. Gregg combats this view energetically,
and says:

*"I can safely say that it is only necessary to make comfort-
able homes in order to procure families that will afford laborers
of the best kind. A large manufacturing establishment located
anywhere in the State, away from a town, and in a healthy
situation, will soon collect around it a population who, however
poor, with proper moral restraints thrown around them, will
soon develop all the elements of good society. Self-respect and
attachment to the place will soon find their way into the minds
of such, while intelligence, morality, and well directed industry
will not fail to acquire position."*

To relieve the extreme poverty and want of the
South it is necessary, according to the teaching of this
report, to lead those who suffer " to regard themselves
as a community;" for this purpose the nuclei of "a
church and a schoolhouse" are essential, to which will
be added, as the work develops, such other stimulants
as "singing and writing schools, itinerant lecturers,"

etc. In short, the power of obtaining, as the result of their labor, "the necessaries of life," "the usual luxuries of country life," or, in two words, which cover and include church, school, music, and lecture, as well as bread, cleanliness, luxuries, and necessities, "comfortable homes."

Mr. Gregg has here indicated, in my opinion, not only the true test of a prosperous people, but the essential condition of prosperity with any people. The mass of men must have in their minds the idea and the hope of a comfortable home as a starting point of respectable industry; must have secured some degree of home comfort as a condition of continued success in their industry.

The present system of American slavery prevents the people at large from having "comfortable homes," in the sense intended by Mr. Gregg. For nine tenths of the citizens, comfortable homes, as the words would be understood by the mass of citizens of the North and of England, as well as by Mr. Gregg, are impossible, and are rendered impossible by the system of slavery.

How?

I believe that all political economists agree in the opinion that either a varied industry within the limits of any given country or district must exist, or that it must enjoy a large export trade, to support a prosperous and happy people. The Slave States would appear to be in the latter condition. Their export of cotton is of great value. It should make comfortable homes

for their people. It does not, because their slavery system interposes to prevent the demand of commerce from having its legitimate effect upon the mass of the people.

Examine almost any rural district of the South, study its history, and it will be seen how it does so.

Take, in the first instance, one of entirely rich soil. Suppose it to be of twenty square miles, with a population of six hundred, all told, and with an ordinarily convenient access by river navigation to market. The whole of the available cotton land in this case will probably be owned by three or four men, and on these men the demand of commerce will have had, let us suppose, its full effect. Their tillage land will be comparatively well cultivated. Their houses will be comfortable, their furniture and their food luxurious. They will, moreover, not only have secured the best land on which to apply their labor, but the best brute force, the best tools, and the best machinery for ginning and pressing, all superintended by the best class of overseers. The cotton of each will be shipped at the best season, perhaps all at once, on a boat or by trains expressly engaged at the lowest rates of freight. It will everywhere receive special attention and care, because it forms together a parcel of great value. The merchants will watch the markets closely to get the best prices for it, and when sold the cash returns to each proprietor will be enormously large. As the expense of raising and marketing cotton are in inverse ratio to the number of hands employed, planters nearly

5

always immediately reinvest their surplus funds in slaves; and as there is a sufficient number of large capitalists engaged in cotton-growing to make a strong competition for the limited number of slaves which the breeding States can supply, it is evident that the price of a slave will always be as high as the product of his labor, under the best management, on the most valuable land, and with every economical advantage which money can procure, will warrant.

But suppose that there are in the district besides these three or four large planters, their families, and their slaves, a certain number, say twenty white families, who do not own slaves. The fact of their being non-slaveholders is evidence that they are as yet without capital. In this case one of two tendencies must soon be developed. Either being stimulated by the high price of cotton they will grow industrious, will accumulate capital and purchase slaves, and owning slaves will require a larger amount of land upon which to work them than they would require for their own labor alone, thus being led to buy out one of the other planters, or to move elsewhere themselves before they have acquired an established improvement of character from their prosperity; or, secondly, they will not purchase slaves, but either expend currently for their own comfort, or hoard the results of their labor. If they hoard they will acquire no increase of comfort or improvement of character on account of the demand. If they spend all their earnings, these will not be sufficient, however profitable their cotton culture may be

supposed, to purchase luxuries much superior to those furnished to the slaves of the planters, because the local demand, being limited to some fifty white families, old and young, in the whole district of twenty square miles, is not enough to draw luxuries to the neighborhood, unless they are brought by special order, and at great expense from the nearest shipping port. Nor is it possible for so small a number of whites to maintain a church or a newspaper, nor yet a school, unless it is one established by a planter, or two or three planters, and really of a private and very expensive character.

Of course this is a somewhat extreme case. As a general rule, accidents of settlement, divisions by inheritance, the resistance of moral or social to economical forces, or other irregular circumstances, will modify in a greater or less degree what is nevertheless the ruling tendency.

Suppose, again, another district in which either the land is generally less productive or the market less easy of access than in the last, or that both is the case. The stimulus of the cotton demand is, of course, proportionately lessened. In this case, equally with the last, the richest soils, and those most convenient to the river or the railroad, if there happens to be much choice in this respect, will assuredly be possessed by the largest capitalists, that is, the largest slaveholders, who may nevertheless be men of but moderate wealth and limited information. If so, their standard of comfort will yet be low, and their demand will consequently take effect

very slowly in increasing the means of comfort, and
rendering facilities for obtaining instruction more accessible to their neighbors. But suppose, notwithstanding the disadvantages of the district in its distance
from market, that their sales of cotton, the sole export of the district, are very profitable, and that the
demand for cotton is constantly increasing. A similar
condition with regard to the chief export of a free labor
community would inevitably tend to foster the intelligence and industry of a large number of people. It
has this effect with only a very limited number of the
inhabitants of a plantation district consisting in large
part as they must of slaves. These laborers may be
driven to work harder, and may be furnished
with better tools for the purpose of increasing the
value of cotton which is to be exchanged for the
luxuries which the planter is learing to demand for
himself but it is for himself and for his family
alone that these luxuries will be demanded. The
wages—or means of demanding home comfort—of
the work men are not at all influenced by the cotton demand, the effect, therefore, in enlarging and
cheapening the local supply of the means of home comfort will be almost inappreciable, while the impulse generated in the planter's mind is almost wholly directed
toward increasing the cotton crop through the labor of
his slaves alone. His demand upon the whites of the
district is not materially enlarged in any way. The
slave population of the district will be increased in
number, and its labor more energetically directed, and

soon the planters will find the soil they possess growing less productive from their increasing drafts upon it.
There is plenty of rich unoccupied land to be had for a
dollar an acre a few hundred miles to the West; still it
is no trifling matter to move all the stock, human,
equine, and bovine, and all the implements and machinery of a large plantation.   Hence, at the same
time, perhaps, with an importation from Virginia of
purchased slaves, there will be an active demand
among the slaveholders for all the remaining land in
the district on which cotton can be profitably grown.
Then sooner or later, and with a rapidity proportionate
to the effect of the cotton demand, the white population of the district divides, one part, consisting of a few
slaveholders, obtains possession of all the valuable cotton land, and monopolizes for a few white families all
the advantages of the cotton demand.   A second part
removes with its slaves, if it possess any, from the
district, while a third continuess to occupy the sand
hills, or sometimes perhaps takes possession of the exhausted land which has been vacated by the large
planters, because they with all their superior skill and
advantages of capital, could not cultivate it longer
with profit.

This class, still ignorant of all luxury, having no
higher aim than to procure the bare means of subsistence, is doomed to remain in a condition thus described
in De Bow's *Review* by a writer "whose name," says
the editor, "has long been illustrious for the services
he has rendered the South":

" All of you must be aware of the condition of the class of people I allude to. What progress have they made in the last hundred years, and what is to be their future condition, unless some mode of employment be devised to improve it ? A noble race of people ! reduced to a condition but little above the wild Indian of the forest, or the European gipsy, without education, and, in many instances, unable to procure the food necessary to develop the natural man. They seem to be the only class of people in our State who are not disposed to emigrate to other countries, while our wealthy and intelligent citizens are leaving us by scores, taking with them the treasures which have been accumulated by mercantile thrift, as well as by the growth of cotton and the consequent exhaustion of the soil." [1]

The population of the district, then, will consist of the large land owners and slave owners, who are now so few in number as to be unnoticeable either as producers or consumers ; of their slaves, who are producers but not consumers (to any important extent), and of this forlorn hope of poor whites, who are, in the eyes of the commercial world, neither producers nor consumers.[2]

To set forth their condition more clearly than I have

[1] Vol. xviii., p. 790.

[2] Mr. Mills's remarks on the condition of India apply, with very slight changes, to portions of the Slave States : " The implements and processes of agriculture are, however, so wretched that the produce of the soil, in spite of its great natural fertility, and a climate highly favorable to vegetation, is miserably small; and the land might be made to yield food in abundance for many more than the present number of inhabitants, without departing from the system of small holdings. But to this the *stimulus* is wanting, which a large town population would afford. That town population again does not grow up because *the few wants and unaspiring spirit* of the cultivators prevent them from attempting to become consumers of *town produce*."

done in the quotations from Southern writers already given in this chapter, is possible only by obtaining the actual statistics of population and trade of a district the soil of which is in great part naturally unproductive, or which has become so through the process I have described. This is difficult, owing not only to the neglect of all the Slave States to obtain statistics of the character now generally required by the legislature of the Free States as a basis of legislative judgment, but owing to the difficulty of finding a region in which the elements of fertility correspond at all closely with the political divisions under which all extant statistics are classified. It would perhaps be desired that I choose for this purpose the counties referred to by Mr. Gregg, but the meagre returns of the National Census appear to be peculiarly untrustworthy with regard to South Carolina, and I prefer to take corresponding counties in Georgia, chiefly because there is a volume of statistics compiled in this State, a special section of which is devoted to the condition of trade in each of its counties, while a comparison is also attempted to be given, from the personal observation of the compiler, of the comparative social, moral, and religious properties of their people. Thus, so far as the plan has been thoroughly executed, an estimate is presented, not only of the ordinary commercial demand of the citizens, but, so to speak, of the state of their intellectual and moral market. I refer to White's *Statistics of Georgia*, a large octavo volume of 700 pages.

The compiler's standard of manners and morals is a local one, and the Northern reader must not understand his language in all cases as he would if it were used by a Northern writer, but taken relatively to one another, the terms by which the people in the different counties are characterized afford significant indications of their condition.

The counties referred to by Mr. Gregg are in the second tier from the sea in South Carolina. I shall give statistics from Mr. White, and other authorities named in the note, [1] with regard to all the second tier counties of Georgia. What of good soil to be brought into cultivation without a heavy expenditure at starting, there was originally in these counties began to be first occupied by whites about 1740. It was not till nearly twenty years after this that slavery obtained the slightest footing in them, and it was not till about thirty years ago that they had begun to seriously deteriorate in production. There is yet some rich land upon the alluvial bottoms of the numerous rivers, which, rising above, pass through these counties toward the ocean ; and here many wealthy planters still re-

[1] The population, following Mr. White, is given in round numbers, from the State census of 1845 ; average personal estate, per family of citizens, reckoned from an official return, published in the *Soil of The South* (Columbus, Georgia, 1852, p. 210), the amount given for each county being divided by one fifth the number of its population (for families). Observations on education and the character of the people, from White's *Statistics of Georgia* (generally in quotations). School, library, and church statistics, in figures, from official United States Census, 1850.

main, owning a large number of slaves, and there has
been recently a considerable increase of production of
some parts owing to the employment of capital in
draining marshes, the riches of which have previously
been considered impregnable. [1]   In general, however,
this whole range of country is now quite barren, and
most of the land at present cultivated will not probably
yield one third as large a crop for the same expenditure
of labor as would fair Mississippi cotton land.   The
slaves formerly owned here have therefore been very
largely transferred westward, and the land they have
worn out is left for the non-slaveholding whites to
make the best of.

As an instructive contrast, I place in an adjoining
column with the statistics of these counties those of
the counties which bound each of them on the east. In
these there is a much larger proportion of rich alluvial
soil, and they contain the famous " sea island " cotton
plantations, as well as the Georgian rice plantations.
The valuable soil is still entirely possessed, as will be
evident, by large planters and slave owners, the usual

---

[1] The presence of these few planters, with their valuable
human property, makes the average nominal wealth of each
white family, at first sight, appear large. If, however, the
slaves had been appraised at only $500 each, which would be
low, they would alone amount in value in some counties to the
sum assigned for the whole personal property of the citizens.
This item is not, therefore, trustworthy, but, in comparing the
coast and second tier counties, it serves to show the great
difference in the average wealth of the citizens of each.   A
similar division of personal estate, as officially returned for the
city of New York, would give $4660 to each family.

monopolizing effect of slavery being in this instance increased by the peculiar local insalubrity of the coast.

SECOND TIER COUNTIES	COAST COUNTIES

Bullock County. (The Central Railroad, the best conducted road in all the South, passes either through this county or close beside its northern boundary, for a distance of fifty miles. It is watered by the Ogeechee and Connauchee and a number of smaller rivers. On the larger rivers there is yet a considerable amount of productive land.)

Bryan County, adjoining Bullock county, on the coast.

Population. Whites, 2000; slaves, 1000. Average amount of property to each white family, $1570. State tax for each white family, $2.95.

Population. Whites, 1000; slaves, 2400. Average amount of property to each white family, $5302, (fourfold what it is in Bullock county.) State tax to each white family, $7.
No statistics of trade, again.

Mr. White omits his usual statistics of trade. Both in this and the adjoining coast county of Bryan, the poor people, as well as the planters, are in the habit of dealing directly with Savannah, as described in *Seaboard Slave States*, and there are probably no established tradesmen in either.

The *soil* is described by Mr. White as generally poor, with some productive "hummock" and river tracts.

Soil. "The soil, under the present system of culture, can not, without rest and manure, be made to produce more than one half as much as when new." This appears to refer particularly to the rice plantations.

SECOND TIER COUNTIES

Education. "No newspapers are taken, and few books read. The school fund was once sufficient to educate many poor children, but owing to bad management it has become exhausted." Thus says Mr. White. The census returns show, however, a public school expenditure of $150 per annum, and a private expenditure of $3000, divided among fifteen schools, which is one for eighty square miles. This is so much better than usual, that, with Mr. White's remarks, I am inclined to think it an error.

Character of the people. "By industry and economy, they manage to supply their wants, which, however, are few. Many rely a great deal on game. * * * As far as temperance is concerned, they are

COAST COUNTIES

Education. There is no academy, and there are no schools, except those supported by the "Poor School Fund," (a State provision for the children of indigent parents.) "The children of the wealthy are either educated by private teachers or sent to school in the more favored portions of the country; [the vicinity of Savannah, where there is a celebrated and well endowed academy, and of Liberty, where there are others, accounts for this;] the population is too sparse to furnish pupils enough to sustain a regular school," (large tracts of land being held by the planters, though wholly unproductive, to prevent the settlement of poor whites near their negroes, as one in this county informed me.) According to the census returns, there were eight schools (one to twenty-five square miles) of all kinds, with an average of twelve pupils each. Total expenditure for each school, $38 per annum.

Character of the people. No remarks.

SECOND TIER COUNTIES

behind the times. Whiskey has its votaries. Those who have attempted to show the citizens the folly and ill consequences of intemperance have been insulted and threatened. Even ministers of our holy religion have publicly denounced the motives and efforts of those who have attempted to form temperance societies."

Religion. "The most numerous [sects] are the Anti-Missionary [hard shell?] Baptists." Ten church edifices; average value, $145. No Sunday-school or other public libraries.

Tatnall County.

Population Whites, 2000; slaves, 600. Average amount of property to each white family, $901.

Capital invested in trade, $4200.

Soil. "Light and sandy, except on the streams, which is stiff."

Education. "Education is neglected." Eight public schools, (1 to 148 square miles) with sixteen pupils each. Annual cost of maintenance of each school, $150. No other

COAST COUNTIES

Religion. The county contains eleven church edifices; average value, $500. No Sunday-school or other public libraries.

Liberty County.

Population. Whites, 2000; slaves, 6000. Average amount of property to each white family, $6330.

State tax to each white family, $10.

Capital invested in trade, $3850.

Soil. "The practice has been to wear out the virgin soils, and clear new lands. * * * Much waste land."

Education. "Excellent schools are found. * * * And it is believed that a greater number of young men from Liberty county graduate from our *colleges* than from any

SECOND TIER COUNTIES

COAST COUNTIES

schools ; no Sunday-school or other libraries.

other section of Georgia." There are five "academies," with an average of nineteen pupils each. Five public schools (1 to 160 square miles), maintained at an average expenditure of $15.40 per annum each. No libraries found in the census canvass of 1849. Mr. White states that the Medway and Newport Library Society had, in 1845, "about seven hundred volumes, in a very bad state of preservation." This library was established by some New England immigrants before the prohibition of slavery was annulled in the province. The early settlers of the county were chiefly from Massachusetts.

Character of the people. "Sober, industrious and hospitable," (phrases applied to every county not specially noted as conspicuous for some vice or virtue of its inhabitants).

Religion. Sixteen church edifices, valued at $938 each. According to Mr. White, however, there are "about thirty churches" in the county.

Character of the people. "Generally upright and virtuous, and they are unsurpassed for the great attention paid to the duties of religion."

Religion. Ten church edifices ; average value, $1200.

Wayne County.

Population. Whites, 930 ; slaves, 350. Average amount

McIntosh County broadest on the sea.

Population. Whites 1300; slaves, 4400. Average

SECOND TIER COUNTIES

of property for each white family, $898.

State tax, $1.23.
Capital invested in trade, $4200.

Soil. "Generally poor, barren pine land ; when manured, will produce about twenty bushels of corn per acre."

Education. "Few schools ;" two academies, (one Baptist, and the other Methodist, probably,) with thirteen pupils between them. Four public schools, (1 to 148 square miles), averaging ten pupils each ; expense of maintenance not returned.

Character of the people. "High for morality and hospitality ;" "poor, but honest." At the seat of justice "are many beautiful pine hills, affording delightful summer residences to the wealthy planters of Glynn," (hence the academical advantages).

Religion. Eight church edifices; average value, $240.

Ware County. (About one fifth of this county is occu-

COAST COUNTIES.

amount of property for each white family, $7287, or eight times as much as in Wayne.
State tax, $2.77.
Capital invested in trade, $1200.

Soil. Poor turpentine pine land in the rear ; on the Altamaha, "of inexhaustible fertility."

Education. One academy, with thirty-eight scholars ; four public schools, twelve and a half miles apart averaging twenty pupils each. Expense of mantaining each school, $78 per annum. "The wealthier classes are highly educated ; but, generally, little interest is felt in the subject of education."

Character of the people. "Like all parts of lower Georgia, the citizens of McIntosh are generally intelligent and hospitable."

Religion. Twelve church edifices ; average value, $1,041.

Camden County. Much the largest part of this

SECOND TIER COUNTIES.

COAST COUNTIES.

pied by the Okefenokee Swamp.)

county, which is L-shaped, with but one arm on the sea, is inland, and unfertile.

Population. Whites, 2000; slaves, 300. Average amount of personal property for each white family, $480.
State tax, $4.05.
Stock in trade, $2200.

Population. Whites, 3000; slaves, 4000. Average amount of personal property for each white family, $4428.
State tax, $13.
"Amount of business done at St. Mary's is about $30,000 per annum," nearly all in lumber, and done by New Englanders. No other trade statistics.

Soil. "Light and tolerably productive."

Soil. "Of celebrated fertility."

Education. "Very little interest is taken in the subject of education." No academies; six public schools (1 to 485 square miles), sixteen pupils each. Wages of teachers, etc., yearly, $41 each school. No Sunday-school or other libraries.

Education. No remarks on education or character by Mr. White. Four public schools (1 to 280 square miles), with seventeen pupils each, maintained at an average expenditure of $290 per annum. Two academies, with forty-five pupils. Five Sunday-school libraries, with one hundred and ten volumes each.

Character of the people. "The citizens are said to be hardy, industrious, and honest." "Much good might be done by the organization of temperance societies."

Character of the people. No remarks.

Religion. Fifteen church edifices, fourteen miles apart,

Religion. Ten churches (five of which are in the town

SECOND TIER COUNTIES

each accommodating one hundred sitters, and valued at $56 each.

COAST COUNTIES

of St. Mary's, a beautiful and healthy village, resorted to by consumptives); average value $850.

I have purposely omitted Effingham county in the above arrangement, because the adjoining coast county of Chatham contains the city of Savannah, an aggregate agency of Northern and foreign merchants, through which is effected the commercial exchanges of a great extent of back country, the population of which can therefore afford no indication as to the point under consideration. Effingham, the county above Chatham, and one of the second tier, is worthy of notice, from some other important exceptional features of its constitution. Owing to the amount of rich soil in the county, along the Savannah River, there is a larger proportion of slaves to the whole population than is usual in the second tier, their number being sixteen hundred against only eighteen hundred whites ; the non-slaveholders, however, appear to possess unusual privileges. There is an academy, with fifty pupils, which Mr. White describes as " a fine school." The public schools, eight in number, are less than eight miles apart, with an average attendance of sixteen pupils. Each school costs one hundred and twelve dollars a year. There are twenty-one churches, less than five miles apart, and valued at over twelve hundred dollars apiece. Mr. White says that honesty and industry are leading characteristics of the people, who, notwithstanding the poverty of the soil, are generally in comfortable circumstances.

The reason of this is partially the close vicinity of Savannah, affording a cash market for a variety of productions and household manufactures, among which, as distinguishing the county from any other in the State, are mentioned fruits, silk, fishing lines, and cow-bells, "the latter," Mr. White is told, " superior to any manufactured in the North or in Europe." But an equally important reason for the better character and condition of the people is to be found in the fact that a majority of them[1] are descendants and heirs of the land of those very early settlers who most strenuously and to the last resisted

---

[1] White's *Statistics*, p. 224.

the introduction of slaves into the colony, being convinced that, if permitted, it would, as they said in their memorials, "prove a scourge" to the poor people who were persuaded to petition for it.[1] It is most gratifying to perceive that all traces of the habits of industry, honesty, and manly self-reliance, in which they thus educated their children, are not wholly lost in the lapse of a century.

To recapitulate the more exact of these statistics :

A large majority of the whole white population resides within the barren counties, of which the slave population is less than one fourteenth that of the aggregate slave population of the whole.

The personal estate of the whites of these upper counties is, on the average, less than one sixth that of the others.

As the wealthy are independent of public schools, *the means of education* are scarcely more available for those who are not rich in one than the other, the school houses being, on an average, ten and a half miles apart in the less populous, thirteen and three quarters miles apart in the more populous.

It is widely otherwise as to *churches*. In the planting counties, there is a house of worship for every twenty-nine white families ; in the poor white counties, one for every one hundred and sixty-two white families. Notwithstanding the fact, that to accommodate all, the latter should be six times as large, their average value is less than one tenth that of the others ; the one being eight hundred and ninety-eight dollars, the other eighty-nine dollars. So wholly do the planters,

---

[1] Hewitt,—; *Seabord Slave States*, vol. ii. p. 167.

in whose hands is the wealth, depend on their factors for direct supplies from without, *the capital invested in trade*, in the coast counties, is but thirty-seven and a half cents to each inhabitant, and in the upper counties it is but one dollar and fifty cents. From the remarks on temperance, it would seem that the most of this capital must be held in the form of whiskey. One "store" in Liberty county, which I myself entered, contained, so far as I could see, nothing but casks, demijohns, decanters, a bag of coffee, a case of tobacco, and some powder and lead, and I believe that nine tenths of the stock in trade referred to in these statistics is of this character. It was mentioned to me by a gentleman who had examined this district with a commercial purpose, that, off the plantations, there was no money in the country—almost literally, no money. The dealings even of the merchants or tradesmen seemed to be entirely by barter. He believed there were many full grown men who had never seen so much as a dollar in money in their lives.

What inducement has capital in railroads or shops or books or tools to move into districts like this, or which are to become like this? Why, rather, I shall be asked, does it not withdraw more completely? Why do not all, who are able, remove from a region so desolate? Why was not its impoverishment more complete, more simultaneous? How is it that any slaveholders yet remain? Mr. Ruffin, president of the Virginia State Agricultural Society, shall answer: [1]

[1] Address before the South Carolina Institute.

"The causes are not all in action at once, and in equal progress. The labors of exhausting culture, also are necessarily suspended as each of the cultivators' fields is successively worn out. And when tillage so ceases, and any space is thus left at rest, nature immediately goes to work to recruit and replace as much as possible of the wasted fertility, until another destroyer, after many years, shall return, again to waste, and in much shorter time than before, the smaller stock of fertility so renewed. Thus the whole territory, so scourged, is not destroyed at one operation. But though these changes and partial recoveries are continually, to some extent, counteracting the labors for destruction, still the latter work is in general progress. It may require (as it did in my native region) more than two hundred years, from the first settlement, to reach the lowest degradation. But that final result is not the less certainly to be produced by the continued action of the causes."

As to the extent to which the process is carried, Mr. Gregg says[1]:

"I think it would be within bounds to assume that the planting capital withdrawn within that period [the last twenty-five years] would, judiciously applied, have drained every acre of swamp land in South Carolina, besides resuscitating the old, worn out land, and doubling the crops—thus more than quadrupling the productive power of the agriculture of the State."

It would be consoling to hope that this planters' capital in the new region to which it is driven were used to better results. Does the average condition of the people of Mississippi and Texas justify such a hope? When we consider the form in which this capital exists, and the change in the mode of its investment which is accomplished when it is transferred from South Carolina, we perceive why it does not.

If we are told that the value of one hundred thousand

[1] Fifth Annual Report to Directors of Graniteville Company.

dollars has been recently transferred from Massachusetts to a certain young township of Illinois, we reasonably infer that the people of this township will be considerably benefited thereby. We think what an excellent saw-mill and grist-mill, what an assortment of wares, what a good inn, what a good school, what fine breeding stock, what excellent seeds and fruit trees, what superior machinery and implements, they will be able to obtain there now, and we know that some of these or other sources of profit, convenience, and comfort to a neighborhood, are almost certain to exist in all capital so transferred. In the capital transferred from South Carolina there is no such virtue— none of consequence. In a hundred thousand dollars of it there will not be found a single mill, or a wagon load of "store goods"; it will hardly introduce to the neighborhood whither it goes a single improvement, convenience, or comfort. At least ninety thousand dollars of it will consist in slaves, and, if their owners go with them, it is hard to see in what respect their real home comfort is greater.

We must admit, it is true, that they are generally better satisfied, else this transfer would not be so unremitting as it is. The motive is the same at the North as at the South, the prospect of a better interest from the capital, and if this did not exist it would not be transferred. Let us suppose that, at starting, the ends of the capitalist are obtained equally in both cases, that a sale of produce is made, bringing in cash twenty thousand dollars; suppose that five thousand

dollars of this is used in each case for the home comfort of the owners, and that as much immediate comfort is attainable with it in the one case as in the other. What, then, is done with the fifteen thousand dollars? At the South, it goes to pay for a further transfer of slaves purchased in the East, a trifle also for new tools. At the North, nearly all of it will go to improvement of machinery of some kind, machinery of transfer or trade, if not of manufacture, to the improvement of the productive value of whatever the original capital had been invested in, much of it to the remuneration of talent, which is thus enabled to be employed for the benefit of many people other than these capitalists— for the home comfort of many people. If five thousand dollars purchased no more comfort in the one case than the other, at starting, in a few years it will purchase double as much. For the fifteen thousand dollars which has gone East in the one case to pay for more labor, will, in the other, have procured good roads and cheap transportation of comforts, or shops and machinery, and thus the cheap manufacture of comforts on the spot where they are demanded. But they who sell the reinforcement of slaves, and to whom comes the fifteen thousand dollars, do they have no increase of home comfort? Taking into consideration the gradual destruction of all the elements of home comfort which the rearing and holding of those slaves has occasioned in the district from which they are sold, it may be doubtful if, in the end, they do. Whither, then, does this capital go? The money comes to the

country from those who buy cotton, and somebody must have a benefit of it. Who? Every one at the South says, when you ask this, it is the Northern merchant, who, in the end, gets it into his own hands, and it is only he and his whom it benefits. Mr. Gregg apparently believes this. He says, after the sentence last quoted from him, describing the transfer of capital to the West from South Carolina:

"But this is not all. Let us look for a moment at the course of things among our mercantile classes. We shall not have to go much further back than twenty-five years to count up twenty-five millions of capital accumulated in Charleston, and which has left us with its enterprising owners, who have principally located in Northern cities. This sum would build factories enough to spin and weave every pound of cotton made in the State, besides making railroads to intersect every portion of the up-country, giving business facilities to the remotest points."

How comes this capital, the return made by the world for the cotton of the South, to be so largely in the hands of Northern men? The true answer is, that what these get is simply their fair commercial remuneration for the trouble of transporting cotton, transporting money, transporting the total amount of home comfort, little as it is, which the South gets for its cotton, from one part of the country to the other (chiefly cotton to the coast, and goods returned instead of money from the coast to the plantations). Is this service over paid? If so, why do not the planters transfer capital and energy to it from the plantations? It is not so. Dispersed and costly labor makes the cost of trade or transfer enormous (as it does the cost of

cotton producing.) It is only when this wealth is transferred to the Free States or to Europe that it gives great results to human comfort. The South, as a whole, has at present no advantage from cotton, even planters but little. The chief result of the demand for it, as far as they are concerned, is to give a fictitious value to slaves.

Throughout the Southwest I found men, who either told me themselves or of whom it was said by others, that they settled where I found them, ten or fifteen years ago, with scarcely any property beyond half a dozen negroes, who were then indeed heavily in debt, but who were now quite rich men, having from twenty to fifty negroes. Nor is this at all surprising, when it is considered that cotton costs nothing but labor, the value of the land, however rich, being too inconsiderable to be taken into account, and that the price of cotton has doubled in ten years. But in what else beside negroes were these rich men better off than when they called themselves poor? Their real comfort, unless in the sense of security against extreme want, or immunity from the necessity of personal labor to sustain life, could scarcely have been increased in the least. There was, at any rate, the same bacon and corn, the same slough of a wagon channel through the forest, the same bare walls in their dwellings, the same absence of taste and art and literature, the same distance from schools and churches and educated advisers, and—on account of the distance of tolerable mechanics, and the difficulty of moving without de-

struction, through such a rough country, anything elaborate or finely finished—the same make-shift furniture. There were, to be sure, ploughs and hoes, and gins and presses, and there were scores of very "likely negroes." Whoever sold such of these negroes as had been bought must have been the richer, it will be said. But let us see:

A large proportion of the negroes were probably bought by traders at forced sales in the older States, sales forced by merchants who had supplied the previous owners of the negroes, and who had given them credit, not on account of the productive value of their property as then situated, but in view of its cash value for sale, that is, of the value which it would realize when applied to cotton on the new soils of the Southwest.

The planters of the Southwest are then, in fact, supplying the deficit of Eastern production, taking their pay almost entirely in negroes. The free West fills the deficit of the free Eastern cereal production, but takes its pay in the manufactured goods, the fish, the oil, the butter, and the importations of the free East.

Virginia planters owning twenty to forty slaves, and nominally worth as many thousand dollars, often seem to live generously, but, according to Northern standards, I do not think that they possess at all equal comforts and advantages for a rationally happy life, with the average of Northern farmers of half that wealth. If they do, they are either supplying slaves for the new cotton fields or living on credit—credit

based on an anticipation of supplying that market.

Of course, it cannot be maintained that no one, while living at the South, is actually richer from the effects of the cotton demand. There are a great many very wealthy men at the South, and of planters, as well as land dealers, negro dealers, and general merchants, but, except in or near those towns which are, practically, colonies of free labor, having constant direct communication and intimate relationship with free countries, the wealth of these more fortunate people secures to them but a small proportion of the advantages which belong to the same nominal wealth anywhere in the Free States, while their number is so small that they must be held of no account at all in estimating the condition of the people, when it is compared with the number of those who are exceedingly destitute, and at whose expense, quite as much as at the expense of their slaves, the wealth of the richer class has been accumulated.

This cannot be rightly deemed extravagant or unjust language. I should not use it if I did not feel satisfied that it was warranted, not only by my own personal observations, but by the testimony of persons whose regard for the pride of the South, whose sympathy with wealthy planters, and whose disposition not to underrate the good results of slavery, if not more sincere than mine, is more certain not to be doubted. I quote, for instance, a single passage from the observations of Mr. Russell, an English gentleman, who, travelling with a special view of studying the agricultural condition and

prospects of the country, was, nevertheless, so much
limited in time that he was obliged to trust, in a great
degree, to the observations of planters for his facts.

" In travelling through a fertile district in any of the Southern States, the appearance of things forms a great contrast to that
in similar districts in the Free States.   During two days' sail on
the Alabama River from Mobile to Montgomery, I did not see
so many houses standing together in any one spot as could be
dignified with the appellation of village : [1] but I may possibly
have passed some at night.   There were many places where
cotton was shipped and provisions were landed, still there were
no signs of enterprise to indicate that we were in the heart of
a rich cotton region.   * * * The planters supply themselves
directly through agents in the large towns, and comparatively
little of the money drawn for the cotton crop is spent in the
Southern States.   Many of the planters spend their incomes by
travelling with their families in the Northern States or in Europe during the summer, and a large sum is required to pay the
hog-raiser in Ohio, the mule-breeder in Kentucky, and, above
all, the Northern capitalists who have vast sums of money on
mortgage over the estates. Dr. Cloud, the editor of the *Cotton
Plant* [Alabama], assured me that after all these items are
paid out of the money received for the whole cotton crop and
sugar crops of the South, there did not remain one fourth part
of it to be spent in the Southern States.   Hence, the Slave
States soon attain a comparatively stationary condition, and,
further, the progress they make is in proportion to the increase of freemen, whose labor is rendered comparatively unproductive, seeing that the most fertile land is occupied by
slaveholders." [2]

I questioned the agent of a large speculation in

[1] Mr. Russell uses the language of England.   There are
several collections of houses on this river bank, the inhabitants
of which would consider it an insult if they should hear such an
humble term as "village" applied to their pseudo towns and
cities.

[2] *North America; Its Agriculture and Climate,* p. 290.

Mississippi with regard to the success of small farmers. In reply he made the following statement, allowing me to take notes of it. I quote from these in order to show that what is true of the Atlantic shore and of the banks of the Alabama is also true of more western and interior districts.

"The majority of our purchasers have been men without capital. To such we usually sell one hundred and sixty acres of land, at from two to three dollars an acre, the agreement being to pay in one, two, and three years, with six per cent. interest. It is very rare that the payments are made when due, and much the largest proportion of this class fail even to pay their interest punctually. Many fail altogether, and quit their farms in about ten years. When crops are generally good, and planters in the same neighborhood make seven bales to a hand, poor people will not make over two bales with their whole family. There is ———— ————, in ———— county, for instance. We sold him one hundred and sixty acres of land in 1843. He has a family of good-sized boys—young men now. For ten years he was never able to pay his interest. He sold from two to four bales a year, but he did not get much for it, and after taking out the cost of bagging and rope, and ginning and pressing, he scarcely ever had two hundred dollars a year coming to him, of which he had to pay his store bills, chiefly for coffee and molasses, sometimes a little clothing—some years none at all. They made their own cloth mostly in the house, but bought sheeting sometimes. He has made one payment on the principal, from a sale of hogs. Almost the only poor people who have kept up to their agreement have been some near ————, since the cotton factory was started there. It is wonderful what a difference that has made, though it's but a picayune affair. People who have no negroes in this country generally raise corn enough to bread them through the year, and have hogs enough ranging in the swamps to supply them with bacon. They do not often buy anything except coffee and molasses and tobacco. They are not generally drunkards, but the men will spend all the money they may have, and get gloriously drunk once or twice a year, at elections or at court time, when they go to the county

town. I think that two bales of cotton a year is as much as is generally made by people who do not own negroes. They are doing well if they net over fifty dollars a year from their labor, besides supplying themselves with corn. A real smart man, who tends his crop well, and who knows how it ought to be managed, can make five bales, almost always. Five bales are worth two hundred and fifty dollars, but it's very rare that a white man makes that. They have not got the right kind of tools, and they don't know how. Their crops are never half tended. If folks generally tended their crops as some do, there would be more than twice as much cotton raised as there is."

With regard to the enlargement of estates by successful planters, having stated what were my impressions, the same gentleman replied that I was entirely right, and gave an instance, as follows, from his personal knowledge :

"J. B. moved into ——— county within my recollection. He has bought out, one after another, and mainly since 1850, more than twenty small land owners, some of them small slaveholders, and they have moved away from the vicinity. I do not know how many negroes he has now, but several hundred, certainly. His surplus must have averaged twenty thousand dollars a year for several years, and, as far as I know, the whole is expended in purchasing negroes or land. He spends no money for anything else in the county, I am sure. It is a common thing to hear a man say, 'J. B. has bought up next to me, and I shall have to quit soon.' He never gets the land alongside of a man that within two years he does not buy him out. In the last ten years I know of but one exception, and that is a man who has shot two of B.'s niggers who were stealing his corn. This man swears he won't sell at any price, and that he will shoot any of J. B.'s niggers whom he catches coming on his place. B.'s niggers are afraid of him, and let him alone. J. B. will pay more for land than it's worth to anybody else, and his negroes are such thieves that nobody can live in comfort on any place adjoining one of his. There are two other men in the county who are constantly buying up

the land around there. The white population of the county is diminishing, and the trade of the place [the county town] is not as good as it was ten years ago."

I am not at liberty to give the name of the above-quoted observer. I will state, however, that he was a Southerner born, and if his narration needs authentica-cation with any reader, I refer to the Hon. C. C. Clay, whose observations [1] will be found to confirm it in all essential particulars, especially in those describing the absorption of small landed properties in large slave estates.

The following description of the social construction of the Western cotton districts I find among the selected matter of a country newspaper. The author is un-known to me, but it is apparent from the context that he writes from personal observation. I quote it, not so much for the additional testimony it offers as for the clearer statement it affords of the tendency I have asserted to exist throughout the rich cotton districts.

"The cotton-growing portion of the valley of the Missis-sippi, the very garden of the Union, is year by year being wrested from the hands of the small farmer and delivered over to the great capitalists. The white yeomen, the class which has contributed more of the blood and devotion, and good sense and enterprise which have made this country what it is than any other, are either forced into the sandy pine-hills or are driven West to clear and prepare the soil for the army of negroes and negro-drivers which forever presses on their heels, to make their industry unprofitable and their life intolerable.

"All the great cotton lands were first opened up by indus-trious settlers, with small means and much energy. No sooner is their clearing made, and their homestead growing into com-fort, than the great planter comes up from the East, with his black horde, settles down on the district, and absorbs and over-

---

[1] *Seaboard Slave States*, vol. ii., p. 223.

runs everything. This is precisely the process which is going on, day by day, over the greater portion of Louisiana and Mississippi. The small farmers, that is to say, the mass of the white population, are fast disappearing. The rich bottom lands of that glorious valley are being concentrated in the hands of large planters, with from one hundred to one thousand negroes. The average number of negroes and average quantity of land belonging to single proprietors is yearly increasing. The wealthier the proprietor himself, the less does he reside on his property, and the more disposed is he to commit it to the care of overseers. In some counties in Mississippi the negroes are twenty times more numerous than the citizens. Whole districts are solely peopled by black 'merchandise,' and some half dozen white drovers. The real 'people' are thus not only deprived of the patrimony which our abolition of the laws of entail and primogeniture was specially intended to secure them; are not only driven off the fairest portions of the soil, like the Scotch Highlanders and the Irish peasantry, but literature and religion are fast disappearing in that portion of this continent on which Providence seems to have intended them to flourish most."

THE DIFFICULTY OF POPULAR EDUCATION

The last sentence, it will be observed, only confirms the opinion quoted from the Superintendent of the Census, at p. 55, an opinion which I have not ventured to express as my own.

In the *Seaboard Slave States*, I declared the impracticability of Mr. Wise's redeeming certain promises he was, when that book was written, freely making to the people of Virginia with regard to the education of the poor whites, unless he was prepared to adopt the emancipation system of Mr. Jefferson with regard to the blacks. I quoted, in evidence of this impracticability, from the county reports printed in the General Report

of the year to the Governor with regard to the working of the then existing educational system of the State. Mr. Wise was elected on those promises. He has occupied the gubernatorial chair four years, and I now take from the report made to Governor Wise himself, November, 1859, extracts of the same kind then given, for several of the considerable slave-holding counties. They are from the remarks of the local commissioners or the superintendents having charge of the expenditure for the education of the indigent.   Comparatively few make any report at all, especially in the slave-holding counties—not nearly as many as in 1852.   I copy all reports with regard to the large slave counties in full, and some instructive notes from counties containing but few slaves.   These are chiefly in the mountain region, and show the influence of the advantages possessed everywhere by the mountain people, as described in the beginning of this chapter, over those living on immediately adjoining plantations, yet the effect upon them of State laws adapted to the necessities of slaveholders is obvious.

BEDFORD

Whites, 13,536 ; slaves, 10,061

" The superintendent states that the benefits of the fund have been extended to a larger number of children than in previous years, but that much remains yet to be done to give to the system the efficiency of which it is capable ; that his observation leads him to believe that a large number of the teachers employed are miserably incompetent, and perhaps better qualified for some other vocation than that of directing the education of the young, and that some other plan ought

to be adopted for the examination of teachers as to their competency before they are employed."

BRUNSWICK

Whites, 4,885 ; slaves, 8,456

"The superintendent regrets that he cannot present in his annual account a full view of the school operations for the year. He has repeatedly urged upon the commissioners the importance of requiring the teachers in their respective districts to render their accounts on or before the 30th of September, but the attainment of that desirable object has not as yet been effected. He can bear cheerful testimony to the capacity, competency, and faithfulness of most of the teachers who are employed to instruct the indigent, and believes that the progress of the pupils is as satisfactory as could be expected under the existing circumstances.

"The present primary school system, whatever may be its defects, has accomplished much good in this county. The benefits conferred thereby on many of the poorer classes of people are not only great but incalculable. The system may be amended ; but as long as Southern society remains as at present constituted, and the white population of the State continues to be sparse, any system that may be devised for the education of the poor will in a great measure prove inefficient."

CULPEPPER

Whites, 5,112 ; slaves, 6,683

"The superintendent states that he has received no synopsis of reports of the commissioners, and he believes that they do not visit the schools very often. Consequently, he has no authority to notice their visits or their observations of the working of the system. The commissioners, however, have promptly attended the meetings of the board, and examined accounts before payment. The superintendent (individually) thinks the system far from being perfect, yet, for the amount expended, it does perhaps as well as any other. To improve the system, would require an immense additional expenditure

to agents, for which the State treasury is but little prepared at the present time."

CUMBERLAND

Whites, 3,082 ; slaves, 6,339.

"The commissioners report that they have found much difficulty in securing the attendance of the children at school ; that many of the teachers are disinclined to take the indigent children, in consequence of the inadequacy of the compensation, and they recommend an increase of the maximum rate of compensation to ten cents a day."

FAIRFAX

Whites, 6,835 ; slaves, 8,250

"The superintendent states, that in some of the districts the teachers refused to dismiss the children when notified of the exhaustion of the district apportionment. In other districts, the commissioners failed to notify the teachers of the insufficiency of funds to continue the children—which must operate a loss to the teachers, though a benefit to the children."

FAYETTE

Whites, 3,780; slaves, 156

"The board report, that the appropriation from the treasury is insufficient to aid in the education of all that really stand in need of assistance from the fund. Those who are the most needy, and at the same time most punctual in their attendance, are the ones for whose benefit we endeavor to apply the funds.

"The superintendent, in his report to the board of school commissioners, says : 'While I would recommend to the board the propriety of having all teachers who apply for schools examined as to their qualifications, I am aware that they are compelled to send to such teachers as are employed by the paying patrons of the school ; but really some plan ought to be adopted to prevent unqualified persons from teaching ; for it is evident, if I be permitted to judge from the accounts presented for payment, that we have many teachers who would not be

injured by taking a few lessons in penmanship and orthography themselves; but I am happy to say to the board that we have some teachers who are eminently qualified to teach. So far as I have been able to observe, there is certainly an increased interest manifested by parents and children on the subject of education and a visible amount of good has been accomplished under the present system. The shortness of the session is one of the greatest objections to the schools. I would, so far as my experience both as teacher and commissioner extends, recommend a general system of free schools; *for while the county is large, and upon first thought one would think sparsely settled, yet the people are generally settled in neighborhoods or settlements sufficiently large and compact to justify the system;* [a mountain county—observe the small proportion of slaves;] and upon the adoption of such a system, I think it would be best for the first few years to teach about six months in the year, including the winter months; and under proper restrictions, I have no doubt but that it would be crowned with success.' "

SPOTSYLVANIA

Whites, 6,894; slaves, 7,481

" The board report that the appropriation from the treasury would not be sufficient, if all the indigent children were sent to school and attended regularly. Some of those entered attend regularly—others not at all. The fault lies in the parents and guardians."

FRANKLIN

Whites, 11,638; slaves, 5,736

" The superintendent regrets to say that it is a difficult thing to get suitable persons to undertake to act as school commissioners, and the duties, when undertaken, are not attended to as they should be; that if a small compensation were allowed, perhaps they would be fulfilled in a better manner."

GLOUCESTER

Whites, 4,290; slaves, 5,887

" The board report that the schools have been visited by some

of the commissioners, and that many of the children have improved very much. The teachers are generally qualified and attentive to their schools. The amount allowed and received for the school fund is entirely insufficient to send all the children entitled to the said fund to school. That they are pleased to say that they have no difficulty now as heretofore in getting the parents to send their children ; hence the large number that attended school the past year.

HANOVER

Whites, 6,539 ; slaves, 8,393

" The board report that they have unshaken confidence in the value of our school system, and would earnestly call upon the Legislature to do all they can constitutionally to increase the fund for this purpose."

"The superintendent reports : The important duty of visiting the districts, inspecting the schools, and making the proper returns to the superintendent, are almost entirely neglected ; and we believe, that partly in consequence of this neglect the proper discrimination between those children who are really proper objects of the State's bounty and those who are not, is lost sight of. I have no hesitation in saying that the small amount of money laid out in our county schools does more good than the same amount expended in any other way, or in any other form of education. There are returns from thirty-four schools, and the teachers are generally believed to be competent."

HENRY

Whites, 5,524 ; slaves, 3,340

" The superintendent states : It will be seen from the foregoing report of the board that there are several blanks which remain unfilled. These blanks cannot be filled with any accuracy, as the commissioners say, which is very true, that they get nothing for their services, and they do not intend to trouble themselves in getting such information as will enable us to fill the blanks in the report. We are, therefore, under the

necessity of forwarding a report which cannot be considered complete.

"I would further remark, that while the commissioners are somewhat remiss in furnishing reports, I do not suppose the children of the county suffer any from that cause, as the teachers' accounts show that the commissioners all send to school fully to the amount allotted their respective districts ; so that the children of the county are getting the full benefit of the fund. The only difficulty is, that the fund is by no means sufficient to educate the indigent children of this county."

HENRICO

Whites, 23,826 ; slaves, 16,109

"The superintendent states that he takes pleasure in reporting the fact that the false pride which has in former years prevented many poor parents from sending their children to school, to be paid for by the State, has been broken down, and that at the present price allowed by the law, most of the teachers in the county are not only willing but anxious to teach the children—so that now the main obstacle in the way of more extended usefulness is the want of sufficient funds. He is of the opinion that nearly double the amount now appropriated might and could be judiciously expended by the board. He thinks the present system is working well, and knows it has and is doing good, and that he has no alteration to suggest except an increase of funds."

ISLE OF WIGHT

Whites, 4,710 ; slaves, 3,395

"The superintendent states that the average attendance of the children at school for the year appears to be only thirty-two and a quarter days, yet were the outstanding claims all paid, it would show quite a different state of things. Those accounts would exhibit an increase of the number of days, while the number of children would only be the same. He has on two or three occasions visited two of the three schools in his district, and was much pleased with the operations of those schools— the teachers being fully competent to the discharge of the im-

portant duties devolving on them.   Had the funds been sufficient, nearly every child in the district could have attended
school through the year."

LANCASTER

Whites, 1,802 ; slaves, 2,640

"The board report that, as a general thing, the schools of
the county are of a higher grade than formerly, and few teachers will take pupils for the price (five cents per day) allowed
by the school commissioners.   The difference between their
charge for tuition and the amount paid by the commissioners is therefore charged to the parents, guardians, or other
friends of the indigent children.   A few very ordinary teachers
may be found who will take pupils at the price allowed by law
out of the funds of the State and county."

MONROE

Whites, 9,062 ; slaves, 1,061

"The committee appointed to report the transactions of the
school commissioners, state that the commissioners have done
as much to promote the interest of the indigent children
as was in their power, laboring as they do under many
disadvantages."

MONTGOMERY

Whites, 6,822 ; slaves, 1,491

"The superintendent has for years complained of the in-
competency of teachers, and he has to regret that the evil is
growing rather than diminishing.   The visiting of schools by
the commissioners has become obsolete."

NANSEMOND

Whites, 5,424 ; slaves, 4,715

"The commissioners have visited their schools during the
year, and are satisfied with the qualifications of their teachers.
The children make very fair improvement.   Children from

eight to eighteen years of age have been admitted to school without regard to sex. The commissioners have not established any new schools, but have sent to those established in different neighborhoods by the people. They have authorized the superintendent to furnish books, paper, etc. The school quota for this county is not sufficient for the education of the indigent children by three or four thousand dollars, if they could be induced to attend school."

NOTTOWAY

Whites, 2,234; slaves, 6,050

"The superintendent is under the necessity of reporting the great want of attention paid to the requirements of the law on the part of school commissioners. Having to make out his account and report almost entirely from teachers' accounts, he is unable consequently to say how many poor children there are in the county who do not attend school, but, from the best information he can get, thinks there are at least sixty or seventy."

TUCKER

Whites,   ; slaves,

"The board report that the insufficiency of the appropriation from the treasury precludes the education of all the poor children of the county, and it is only the most needy that can be sent to school."

WYTHE

Whites, 9,618; slaves, 2,185

"The board report that the funds are insufficient to send all the poor children for the whole time; that their object has been to send all a greater or less time, proportioned to their means."

WOOD

White, 9,008; slaves, 375

"The superintendent congratulates the board upon the advanced condition of the schools of the county generally.

"In reference to the general system of education, as pursued under the present arrangement of Virginia, although it is liable to some defects and objections, yet if properly and efficiently attended to and carried out by the commissioners, in selecting good and competent teachers, and in a just and equitable distribution of the funds for the education of the indigent children in all the neighborhoods of the county, it is the best that can be devised."

THE QUESTION OF COTTON SUPPLY

Mr. Russell, although he clearly sees the calamity of the South, fully accepts the cotton planter's opinion, that, after all, the system of slavery is a necessary evil attending upon the great good of cheap cotton. He says: "If the climate had admitted of the growing of cotton on the banks of the Ohio, we should have seen that slavery possessed as great advantages over free labor in the raising of this crop as it does in that of tobacco." If this is so, it is important that it should be well understood why it is so as precisely as possible.

In his *Notes on Maryland*, Mr. Russell (p. 141) says: "Though a slave may, under very favorable circumstances, cultivate twenty acres of wheat and twenty acres of Indian corn, he cannot manage more than two acres of tobacco. The cultivation of tobacco, therefore, admits of the concentration of labor, and thus the superintendence and management of a tobacco plantation will be more perfect and less expensive than a corn one." And this is the only explanation he offers of the supposed advantage of slave labor in the cultivation of tobacco (and of consequence in the cultivation of cotton.) The chief expense of raising corn

is chargeable to planting and tillage, that of tobacco to
the seed-bed, the transplanting and nursing of the
young plants (which is precisely similar to the same
operation with cabbages), the hand-weeding, the hoeing after the plant has "become too large to work
without injuring the leaves by the swingle-trees of a
horse-plough"[1]; "the topping," "the suckering," the
selection and removal of valueless leaves, and "the
worming," all of them, except hoeing, being operations which can be performed by children and child-
bearing women, as they usually are in Virginia.[2]

The chief expense of raising cotton, as of corn, is
that of planting and tillage. The principal difference
between the method of tillage of cotton and that of
corn is occasioned by the greater luxuriance of weeds
in the Southern climate and the slow growth of the
cotton plant in its early stages, which obliges the tillage process to be more carefully and more frequently
performed. For this reason, the area of cotton cultivated by each laborer is less than of corn. The area
of corn land to a hand is, however, very much over-
estimated, in my opinion, by Mr. Russell. On the other
hand, the only mention he makes of the area of cotton
land to a hand (being the statement of a negro) would
lead to the conclusion that it is often not over three
acres, and that five acres is extraordinary. Mr. De
Bow says,[3] in an argument to prove that the average

[1] De Bow, vol. iii., p. 342.

[2] See De Bow's *Resources*, art. "Tobacco."

[3] Vol. i., p. 175, *Resources*.

production per acre is over-estimated, "In the real cotton region, perhaps the average number of acres per hand is ten."

Mr. Russell observes of worming and leafing tobacco : "These operations can be done as well, and consequently as cheaply, by women and children as by full grown men" (page 142). After reading Mr. Russell's views, I placed myself, through the kindness of Governor Chase, in communication with the Ohio Board of Agriculture, from which I have obtained elaborate statistics, together with reports on the subject from twelve presidents or secretaries of county agricultural societies, as well as from others. These gentlemen generally say that a certain amount of labor given to corn will be much better repaid than if given to tobacco. "Men are worth too much for growing corn to be employed in strolling through tobacco fields, looking for worms, and even women can, as our farmers think, find something better to do about the house." Children, too, are thought to be, and doubtless are, better employed at school in preparing themselves for more profitable duties, and this is probably the chief reason why coarse tobacco [1] cannot be cultivated with

[1] In my Notes on Eastern Virginia, it was mentioned that a tobacco planter informed me that he could not raise the finer sorts of tobacco with profit, because he could not make his slaves take pains enough with it; and in certain localities in Ohio, having a favorable soil for the production of fine or high priced tobacco, it appears that free labor is engaged more profitably in the cultivation of tobacco than in the cultivation of corn. It is the same in parts of Connecticut and of Massachusetts. Except in these limited districts, however, it is found

as much profit as corn in Ohio, while the want of intelligent, self-interested labor is the reason why the
corn-field, among the broad blades of which a man will
work during much of its growth in comparative ob-
scurity, cannot be cultivated with as much profit on
soils of the same quality in Virginia as in Ohio. In
short, a class of laborers, which are good for nothing
else, and which but for this would be an intolerable
burden upon those who are obliged to support them,
can be put to some use in raising tobacco, and, therefore, coarse tobacco continues to be cultivated in some
of the principal slave holding counties of Virginia. But
this class of laborers is of no more value in cotton
culture than in corn culture. Mr. De Bow says: ''The
Southwest, the great cotton region, is newly settled,
and the number of children, out of all proportion, less
than in negroes [regions?] peopled by a natural growth
of population.[1] Weak women and weak children are,
in fact, not at all in demand for cotton culture, the
cotton planter's inquiry being only for 'prime boys,'
or 'A 1 field hands.' ''

Thus, in every way, cotton culture, in my judgment,
more resembles corn culture than it does tobacco culture. The production of corn is larger in the aggregate,
is considerably larger per man engaged in its cultivation, and is far larger per acre in Ohio than in

---

that the labor of Ohio, as of Connecticut and Massachusetts, is
more profitably directed to the cultivation of corn (maize) and
other crops than of tobacco.

[1] *Resources*, p. 175.

Virginia.[1] I should, therefore, be inclined to reverse
Mr. Russell's statement, and to say that if the climate
had admitted of the growing of cotton on both banks
of the Ohio, we should have seen that free labor possessed as great advantages over slavery in the cultivation
of cotton as of corn.

Mr. Russell echoes also the opinion, which every
cotton planter is in the habit of urging, that the production of cotton would have been comparatively insignificant in the United States if it had not been for
slave labor. He likewise restricts the true cotton region
within much narrower limits than are usually given to
it, and holds that the slave population must soon in a
great measure be concentrated within it. As these conclusions of a scientific traveller unintentionally support
a view which has been lately systematically pressed
upon manufacturers and merchants both in Great

[1] Virginia, with 10,360,135 acres of improved land, produced,
according to the last census returns,

> 35,254,319 bushels of corn,
> 56,803,227 pounds of tobacco.

Ohio, with 9,851,493 acres of improved land, produced

> 59,078,695 bushels of corn,
> 10,454,449 pounds of tobacco.

The aggregate value of these two products alone, at present
New York prices, would be

> Ohio.........$5,127,223,565
> Virginia.......$3,564,639,385

Actual crops per acre, on the average, as returned by the
marshals for 1849–50 (*Census Compilation*, p. 178):

	Corn.	Tobacco.
Ohio........	36 bushels.....	730 pounds.
Virginia.....18	"	630 "

Britain and the Free States, namely, that the perpetuation of slavery in its present form is necessary to the perpetuation of a liberal cotton supply, and also that the limit of production in the United States must be rapidly approaching, and consequently that the tendency of prices must be rapidly upward, the grounds on which they rest should be carefully scrutinized.

Mr. Russell says in a paragraph succeeding the words just now quoted with regard to the supposed advantages of slave labor in raising tobacco :

"The rich upland soils of the cotton region afford a profitable investment for capital, even when cultivated by slaves left to the care of overseers. The natural increase of the slaves, from two to six per cent., goes far to pay the interest of the money invested in them. The richest soils of the uplands are invariably occupied by the largest plantations, and the alluvial lands on the banks of the rivers are so unhealthy for white laborers that the slave owners occupy them without competition. Thus the banks of the Western rivers are now becoming the great cotton-producing districts. Taking these facts into consideration, it appears that the quantity of cotton which would have been raised without slave labor in the United States would have been comparatively insignificant to the present supply." [1]

The advantages of slave labor for cotton culture seem from this to have been predicated mainly upon the unwholesomeness to free or white laborers of the best cotton lands, especially of the alluvial lands on the banks of rivers. Reference is made particularly to " the county of Washington, Mississippi State, [which] lies between the Yazoo and Mississippi rivers. * * * The soil is chiefly alluvial, though a considerable portion is swampy and liable to be flooded."

[1] *North America* ; *Its Climate*, etc., p. 286.

Mr. Russell evidently considers that it is to this swampy condition, and to stagnant water left by floods, that the supposed insalubrity of this region is to be chiefly attributed.   How would he explain, then, the undoubted salubrity of the bottom lands in Louisiana, which are lower than those of the Mississippi, exposed to a more southern sun, more swampy, and which were originally much more frequently flooded, but having been dyked and " leveed,"are now inhabited by a white population of several hundred thousand ?   I will refer to the evidence of an expert :

" Heat, moisture, animal and vegetable matter, are said to be the elements which produce the diseases of the South, and yet the testimony in proof of the health of the banks of the lower portion of the Mississippi River is too strong to be doubted.   Here is a perfectly flat alluvial country, covering several hundred miles, interspersed with interminable lakes, lagunes and jungles, and still we are informed by Dr. Cartwright, one of the most acute observers of the day, that this country is exempt from miasmatic disorders, and is extremely healthy.   His assertion has been confirmed to me by hundreds of witnesses, and we know, from our own observation, that the population presents a robust and healthy appearance." (Statistics are given to prove a greater average length of life for the white race in the South than in the North.)—*Essay on the Value of Life in the South*, by Dr. J. C. Nott, of Alabama.[1]

The unacclimated whites on the sea coast and on the river and bayou banks of the low country, between which and the sea coast there is much intercommunication, suffer greatly from certain epidemic, contagious, and infectious pestilences.   This, however, only renders the fact that dense settlements of whites have been

[1] De Bow's *Resources*.   See *Seaboard Slave States*, vol. ii., pp. 95 and 234, for further Southern evidence.

firmly established upon them, and that they are remarkably exempt from miasmatic disease, one of more value in evidence of the practicability of white occupation of the upper bottom lands. There are strong grounds for doubting the common opinion that the negroes at the South suffer less from local causes of disease than whites.[1] They may be less subject to epidemic and infectious diseases, and yet be more liable to other fatal disorders than whites. The worst climate for unacclimated whites of any town in the United States is that of Charleston. (This, together with the whole of the rice coast, is clearly exceptional in respect to salubrity for whites.) It happens fortunately that the most trustworthy and complete vital statistics of the South are those of Charleston. Dr. Nott, commenting upon these, says that the average mortality, during six years, has been, of blacks alone, one in forty-four ; of whites alone, one in fifty-eight. "This mortality," he adds, "is perhaps not an unfair test, as the population during the last six years has been undisturbed by emigration, and acclimated in greater proportion than at any previous period." If the comparison had been made between native negroes and native or acclimated whites alone, it would doubtless show the climate to be still more unfavorable to negroes.[2]

[1] *See Seaboard Slave States.* Vol. ii., p. 303

[2] Dr. Barton, of New Orleans, in a paper read before the Academy of Science of that city, says : " The class of diseases most fatal in the South are mainly of a '*preventible* ' nature,

Upon the very district to which Mr. Russell refers, as offering an extreme case, I quote the testimony of a Mississippi statistician :

"The cotton planters, deserting the rolling land, are fast pouring in upon the 'swamp.' Indeed, the impression of the sickliness of the South generally has been rapidly losing ground, [*i. e.* among the whites of the South] for some years back, and that blessing [health] is now sought with as much confidence on the swamp lands of the Yazoo and the Mississippi as among the hills and plains of Carolina and Virginia."—(*De-Bow's Resources,*" vol. ii., p. 43.)

Dr. Barton says :

" In another place I have shown that the direct temperature of the sun is not near so great in the South, (during the summer), as it is at the North. I shall recur to this hereafter. In fact, the climate is much more endurable, all the year round, with our refreshing breezes, and particularly in some of the more elevated parts of it, or within one hundred miles of the coast, both in and out of doors, at the South than at the North, which shows most conspicuously the folly of the annual summer migrations, to pursue an imaginary mildness of temperature, which is left at home."

Mr. Russell assumes that slave labor tends, as a matter of course, to the formation of large plantations, and that free labor can only be applied to agricultural

---

and embraces fevers and intestinal diseases, and depends mostly on conditions under the control of man, as drainage, the removal of forest growth—of personal exposure and private hygiene. The climate further north is too rigid the greater part of the year, for personal exposure to the open air, so essential to the enjoyment of health, and when the extremes are great and rapid, another class of maladies predominate—the pulmonary, as well as others arising from crowding, defective ventilation and filth—exacting preventive measures from the public authorities with as much urgency as the worst fevers of the South."

operations of a limited scope. Of slaves, he says:
"Their numbers admit of that organization and division
of labor which render slavery so serviceable in the
culture of cotton." I find no reason given for this assumption, except that he did not himself see any
large agricultural enterprises conducted with free labor,
while he did see many plantations of fifty to one hundred slave hands. The explanation, in my judgment,
is that the cultivation of the crops generally grown in
the Free States has hitherto been most profitable when
conducted on the "small holding" system [1]; the cultivation of cotton is, as a general rule, more profitable
upon the "large holding" system.[2] Undoubtedly
there is a point below which it becomes disadvantage-
ous to reduce the farm in the Free States, and this
varies with local circumstances. There is equally a
limit beyond which it is acknowledged to be unprofitable to enlarge the body of slaves engaged in cotton cultivation under one head. If cotton were to be cultivated
by free labor, it is probable that this number would be
somewhat reduced. I have no doubt that the number
of men on each plantation, in any case, would on an
average, much nearer approach that which would be

[1] Corn has been considered an exception, and there are
probably larger corn fields in Indiana than cotton fields in
Mississippi.

[2] I believe that plantations or agricultural operations devoted
to a single crop are, as a general rule, profitable in proportion
to their size in the Free States, unless indeed the market is a
small one and easily overstocked, which is never the case with
the cotton market.

most economical, in a free labor cotton growing country
than in a country on which the whole dependence of
each proprietor was on slaves. Is not this conclusion
irresistible when we consider that the planter, if he
needs an additional slave hand to those he possesses,
even if temporarily, for harvesting his crop, must, in
most cases, employ at least a thousand dollars of capital to obtain it ?

Mr. Russell has himself observed that—

"The quantity of cotton which can be produced on a [slave-
worked] plantation is limited by the number of hands it can
turn into the field during the picking or harvesting of the crop.
Like some other agricultural operations, this is a simple one,
though it does not admit of being done by machinery, as a certain amount of intelligence must direct the hand."

The same is true of a wheat farm, except that much
more can be done by machinery, and consequently the
extraordinary demand for labor at the wheat harvest
is much less than it is on a cotton plantation. I have
several times been on the Mississippi plantations during picking time, and have seen how everything black,
with hands, was pressed into severe service; but, after
all, I have often seen negroes breaking down, in preparation for re-ploughing the ground for the next crop,
acres of cotton plants, upon which what appeared to
me to be a tolerable crop of wool still hung, because it
had been impossible to pick it. I have seen what was
confessed to be many hundred dollars' worth of cotton
thus wasted on a single Red River plantation. I much
doubt if the harvest demand of the principal cotton
districts of Mississippi adds five per cent. to their field

hand force. In Ohio there is a far larger population ordinarily engaged in other pursuits which responds to the harvest demand. A temporary increase of the number of agricultural laborers thus occurs of not less than forty per cent. during the most critical period.

An analogous case is that of the vintage in the wine districts of France. In some of these the "small holding" or *parcellement* system is carried to an unfortunate extreme under the influence of what are perhaps injudicious laws. The parcels of land are much smaller, on an average, than the smallest class of farms ordinarily cultivated by free labor in the United States. But can any one suppose that if the slave labor system, as it exists in the United States, prevailed in those districts, that is to say, if the proprietors depended solely on themselves, their families, and their regular servants, as those of Mississippi must, at the picking time, there would not be a disastrous falling off in the commerce of those districts? Substitute the French system, unfortunate as in some respects it is, for the Mississippi system in cotton growing, and who will doubt that the commerce of the United States would be greatly increased?

Hop picking and cotton picking are very similar operations. The former is the more laborious, and requires the greater skill. What would the planters of Kent do if they had no one but their regulars to call upon at the harvest season? As it is, the population in many parishes in Kent I suppose to be quadrupled in picking time.

I observed this advantage of the free labor system exemplified in Western Texas, the cotton fields in the vicinity of the German village of New Braunfels having been picked, when I saw them, far closer than any I had before seen, in fact, perfectly clean, having been undoubtedly gleaned by the poor emigrants. I was told that some mechanics made more in a day, by going into the field of a slave owner and picking side by side with his slaves, being paid by measure, than they could earn at their regular work in a week. The degree of intelligence and of practice required to pick to advantage was found to be very slight, less very much than in any single operation of wheat harvesters. One woman was pointed out to me who had, in the first year she had ever seen a cotton field, picked more cotton in a day than any slave in the county.

I am reminded, as this page is about to be stereotyped, by observing the letter of a cotton planter in the New Orleans *Price Current*, of another disadvantage for cotton production, of slave labor, or rather of the system which slavery induces. In the *Texas Journey*, I stated that I was informed by a merchant that the cotton picked by the free labor of the Germans was worth from one to two cents a pound more than that picked by slaves in the same township, by reason of its greater cleanliness. From the letter referred to, I make the following extracts:

"DEAR SIR : * * * There are probably no set of men engaged in any business of life who take as little pains and care to inform themselves with regard to the character and quality

of their marketable produce as the cotton planter.   Not one in
a thousand knows, nor cares to know, whether the cotton he
sends to market is ordinary, good ordinary, or middling.   Not
one in a hundred spends one hour of each day at his gin in
ginning season ; never sees the cotton after it is gathered, unless he happens to ride near the scaffold and looks from a distance of a hundred yards, and declares the specimen very white
and clean, when, perhaps, it, on the contrary, may be very
leafy and dirty. * * *

"I have often seen the hands on plantations picking cotton
with sacks that would hardly hold stalks, they were so torn
and full of holes ; these sacks dragging on the ground and
gathering up pounds of dirt at every few steps.   The baskets,
too, were with scarcely any bottoms remaining, having been
literally worn out, the cotton lying on the ground.   Indeed,
some overseers do not forbid the hands emptying their cotton
on the ground when their sacks are full, and they some distance from their baskets.   When this cotton is taken up, some
dirt must necessarily come with it.   When gathering in wet
weather, the hands get into their baskets with muddy feet, and
thus toss in some pounds of dirt, in this way making their task
easier.   These things are never, or rarely seen by the proprietor ; and, consequently, when his merchant writes him that his
cotton is a little dusty, he says how can it be? you are surely
mistaken.

"Now, sir, for all this there is one simple, plain remedy ; let
the planter spend his time in ginning season at his gin ; let
him see every load of cotton as it comes from the field and before it goes through the gin.   But, says the man of leisure, the
gin is a dirty, dusty place.   Yes, sir, and always will be so,
until you remedy the evil by staying there yourself.   You say
your overseer is hired to do this dirty work.   *Your overseer is
after quantity, sir, and the more extra weight he gets in your
cotton, the more bales he will have to brag of having made at
the end of the year.   Don't trust him at the gin.* * * *

" Probably he has a conditional contract with his employer :
*gets so many dollars for all he makes over a certain number of
bales; thus having every inducement to put up as much leaf and
dirt, or, if he is one of the dishonest kind, he may add stones,
if they should abound in the neighborhood.*

"Why will not the cotton planter take pride in his own

production? The merchant prides himself on his wares; the mechanic on the work of his hands. All seem to pride themselves on the result of their labor except the cotton planter." * * *

It cannot be admitted that the absence in the Free States of that organization and division of labor in agriculture which is found on a large slave-worked plantation is a necessity attending the use of free labor. Why should it be any more impossible to employ an army of free laborers in moving the ground with an agricultural design than with the intention of constructing a canal or a road, if it were profitable to so employ the necessary capital? A railroad contractor in one of the best cotton districts of the United States told me, that having begun his work with negroes, he was substituting Irish and German laborers for them as rapidly as possible, with great advantage, (and this near midsummer). But if I were convinced with Mr. Russell upon this point, I should still be inclined to think that the advantages which are possessed in a free-labor state of society equally by the great hop planters at picking time and the *petits proprietaries* at vintage, which are also found in our own new States by the wheat farmer, and which are not found under the present system anywhere at the South, for cotton picking, would of themselves be sufficient to turn the scale in favor of the free-labor cotton grower.

The errors of the assumption upon which the opinion is based by Mr. Russell, that slave labor is essential or important to sustain cotton production in the

United States, is, I trust, apparent. The more common and popular opinion is, that the necessary labor of cotton tillage is too severe for white men in the cotton-growing climate. As I have said before, I do not find the slightest weight of fact to sustain this opinion. The necessary labor and causes of fatigue and vital exhaustion attending any part or all of the process of cotton culture does not compare with that of our July harvesting ; it is not greater than attends the cultivation of Indian corn in the usual New England method. I have seen a weakly white woman the worse for her labor in the cotton field, but never a white man, and I have seen hundreds of them at work in cotton fields under the most unfavorable circumstances, miserable, dispirited wretches, and of weak muscle, subsisting mainly, as they do, on corn bread.   Mr. De Bow estimates one hundred thousand white men now engaged in the cultivation of cotton, being one ninth of the whole cotton force (numerically) of the country.[1]   I have just seen a commercial letter from San Antonio, which estimates that the handful of Germans in Western Texas will send ten thousand bales of cotton, the production of their own labor, to market this season. If it should prove to be half this, it must be considered a liberal contribution to the needed supply of the year, by those who, following Mr. Russell, have considered Western Texas out of the true cotton region, and taking the truth of the common planters' assertion for granted, have thought Africans, working under physi-

[1] *Resources*, vol. i., p. 175.

cal compulsion, the only means of meeting the demand which could be looked to in the future of the United States.

It would not surprise me to learn that the cultivation of cotton by the German settlers in Texas had not, after all, been as profitable as its cultivation by the planters employing slaves in the vicinity. I should attribute the superior profits of the planter, if any there be, however, not to the fitness of the climate for negro labor, and its unfitness for white labor, but to the fact that his expenses for fencing, on account of his larger fields and larger estate, are several hundred per cent. less than those of the farmer; to the fact that his expenses for tillage, having mules and ploughs and other instruments to use at the opportune moment, are less than those of the farmer, who, in many cases, cannot afford to own a single team; to the fact that he has, from experience, a better knowledge of the most successful method of cultivation ; to the fact that he has a gin and a press of his own in the midst of his cotton fields, to which he can carry his wool at one transfer from the picking ; by which he can put it in order for market expeditiously, and at an expense much below that falling upon the farmer, who must first store his wool, then send it to the planter's gin and press and have it prepared at the planter's convenience, paying, perhaps, exorbitantly therefor ; and finally, to the fact that the planter deals directly with the exporter, while the farmer, the whole profit of whose crop would not pay his expenses in a journey to the coast, must transfer his bale or two to the exporter

through two or three middle-men, carrying it one bale at a time, to the local purchaser. Merchants will never give as good prices for small lots as for large. There are reasons for this which I need not now explain. I consider, in short, that the disadvantages of the farmer in growing cotton are of the same nature as I have before explained [1] with those which long ago made fire-wood of hand-looms, and paupers of those who could be nothing else but hand-loom weavers, in Massachusetts. Exactly how much is gained by the application of labor with the advantage of capital and combination of numbers over its isolated application as directed by individuals without capital in a slave-holding region, I cannot estimate, but no one will doubt that it is considerable. Nevertheless, in all the cotton climate of the United States, if a white farmer has made money without slaves, it will be found that it has been, in most cases, obtained exclusively from the sale of cotton. If cotton is a plant the cultivation of which by free or white labor is especially difficult, how is it that, with the additional embarrassments arising from a lack of capital, his gains are almost exclusively derived from his cotton crop?

But I may be asked, if combination is what is needed to make cotton a source of more general prosperity at the South, why is there no such thing as a joint-stock cotton plantation in Mississippi, as there are joint-stock cotton mills in Massachusetts, the stock in which is in large part owned by those employed in them? I ask, in reply, how is it that the common way of obtain-

[1] See Vol. i., p. 131.

ing bread stuffs in northern Alabama is to sow three pecks
of seed wheat on hard stubble ground, plough it under with unbroken bullocks, led with a rope, and a bull-
tongue plough, and finally to garner rarely so much as
six bushels from an acre.   How is it that while in Ohio
the spinning-wheel and hand-loom are curiosities, and
homespun would be a conspicuous and noticeable material of clothing, half the white population of Mississippi still dress in homespun, and at every second house
the wheel and loom are found in operation?   The same
influences which condemn the majority of free laborers
in Alabama to hand-looms, homespun, and three hundred pounds of wheat to the acre as the limit of production, also condemn them to isolated labor, poor soil,
poor tools, bad management, "bad luck," small crops
and small profits in cotton culture.

The following passages from a letter published in the
New York *Times* present convincing evidence that it
is no peculiarity of the Western Texas climate, but
only the exceptional social condition with which its
people are favored, that enables free white labor to be
employed in increasing the cotton production of the
country.   I have ascertained that the author of the
letter is known to the editor of the *Times*, and is
esteemed a gentleman of veracity and trustworthy
judgment.

"I am well acquainted with Eastern Mississippi, south of
Monroe County, and there are few settlements where my name
or face is unknown in the following counties, over the greater
part of which I have ridden on horseback, to-wit: Loundes,
Oktibleha, Choctaw, Carroll, Attalla, Winston, Noxubee, Kem-

per, Nashoba, Leake, Scott, Newton, Lauderdale, Clarke, Smith, and Jasper. After four years' travel through these counties, transacting business with great numbers of their inhabitants, stopping at their houses, conversing much with them, and viewing their mode of living, I unhesitatingly answer that white men can and do labor in the cotton field, from Christmas to Christmas following; and that there, as elsewhere, prudence, industry, and energy find their universal reward, success, and wealth.

"In the counties of Choctaw, Winston, Nashoba, Newton, and Smith, there are very few large plantations; most of those having slaves holding but two or three, while those who own none are in the majority; yet these are all cotton-growing counties, and the staple of their cotton, poor as their lands are, is equal to the average sold in the Mobile market. Where the young farmer is enterprising and go-ahead, his cotton is usually superior. * * *

"The rich lands where white labor, even in small numbers, might be profitable, are either in the hands of large planters, or too heavily timbered for a single man. The only thing now preventing any poor white man in the South from gaining a fair competence, and even attaining wealth, is his own lazinesss, shiftlessness, and ignorance; for the small planters in the counties I have mentioned are deplorably ignorant. * * *

"There is one case I remember, which is to the point; the man lives in Choctaw County, and was born in Georgia. He does not own a negro, but has two boys, one sixteen, the other twelve. With the assistance of these boys, and the most imperfect agricultural implements, he made twenty-two bales of cotton, year before last, plenty of corn, and sufficient small grain for himself and family, although the season was more than ordinarily bad in his neighborhood, while many of his neighbors, with five or six slaves, did not exceed him, and some made even less. He went on to his place without ten dollars in his pocket, gave his notes for eight hundred dollars, payable in one, two, and three years' time, with interest at six per cent per annum, and the ensuing year he purchased another one hundred and sixty acres for seven hundred and fifty dollars, also on time. This man is however far more intelligent and progressive in farming than those about him; he does not plant as did his grandfather, because his father did so, but endea-

vors to improve and is willing to try an experiment occasionally.

"In my own county, in Alabama, there is a woman whose husband died shortly after the crop was planted, leaving her without a single servant, and no assistance except from a little son of twelve years of age : yet she went into the field, plowed and picked her cotton, prepared her ground for the coming crop, and raised a second crop thereon."

My conclusion, from the various evidences to which I have referred, would be a widely different one from Mr. Russell's, from that which is generally thought to prevail with our leading capitalists, merchants, and manufacturers, and from that which seems to have been accepted by the Cotton Supply Associations of Liverpool and Manchester.   It is this: that there is no physical obstacle in the way of our country's supplying ten bales of cotton where it now does one.   All that is necessary for this purpose is to direct to the cotton-producing region an adequate number of laborers, either black or white, or both.   No amalgamation, no association on equality, no violent disruption of present relations is necessary.   It is not even requisite that both black and white should work in the cotton fields. It is necessary that there should be more objects of industry, more varied enterprises, more general intelligence among the people, and especially that they should become or desire to become richer, more comfortable, than they are.

The simple truth is, that even if we view in the brightest light of Fourth of July patriotism, the character of the whites of the cotton-producing region, and the condition of the slaves, we cannot help seeing that, commercially speaking, they are but in a very

small part a civilized people. Undoubtedly a large
number of merchants have a profitable business in supplying civilized luxuries and conveniences to the
South. The same is true of Mexico, of Turkey, of
Egypt, and of Russia. Silk, cloth and calico, shoes,
gloves and gold watches, were sold in some quantity in
California before its golden coffers were forcibly opened
ten years ago. The Southern supply to commerce and
the Southern demand of commerce is no more what it
should be, comparing the resources of the South with
those of other lands occupied by an active civilized
community, than is that of any half civilized community, than was that of California. Give the South a
people moderately close settled, moderately well-informed, moderately ambitious, and moderately industrious, somewhat approaching that of Ohio, for instance,
and what a business it would have! Twenty double-track
railroads from the Gulf to the Lakes, and twenty lines of
ocean steamers, would not sufficiently meet its requirements. Who doubts, let him study the present business of Ohio, and ask upon what in the natural resources of Ohio, or its position, could, forty years ago,
a prediction of its present wealth and business have
been made, of its present supply and its present demand have been made, which would compare in value
with the commercial resources and advantages of
position possessed to-day by any one of the Western
cotton states.[1]

[1] Some one can render a service to civilization by publishing
precisely what feudal rights, so called, were abolished in large

REMEDIAL MEASURES

Mr. Gregg's scheme, which I have before described, as a simple, common-sense method of palliating the wretchedness of the poor of his own district, by endeavoring to make practicable to them the acquisition of " home comforts." That it can afford only a palliation will be obvious if we consider how much capital would be needed to make it a remedy, having a general application. So large a part of the whole population consists of slaves, whose demand for manufactured goods would be supplied by a small number of operatives, the factories would be required to send their goods to a distance for purchasers. Mr. Gregg acknowledges that the manufacture of the coarse goods, such as are chiefly required by slaves, and which near the factory displace the common home-spun and woven cloth formerly worn by the majority of the free people, has been already overdone. He estimates the white population of South Carolina alone, " who ought to work and who do not, or who are so employed as to be wholly unproductive to the State," at one hundred and twenty-five thousand. If they were all collected, as he proposes, they would operate (upon his own data) five million spindles.   In

---

parts of Germany and Hungary in 1848, and what results to the commerce of the districts affected the greater freedom and impulse to industry arising therefrom has had. If I am rightly informed, trade, in many cases, both export and import, has already much more than quadrupled in value, thousands of peasants now demanding numerous articles and being able to pay for them, which before only a few score or hundred proprietors were expected to buy.

Massachusetts, with all its railroads, foundries, quarries, and machine shops, it is usual to reckon the plant cost of a factory of the character proposed by Mr. Gregg at twenty-five dollars a spindle.   Thus, to put at work, on Mr. Gregg's plan, merely that portion of the population of South Carolina who at present are pure vagrants, and attempting nothing directly for those who barely earn their own means of subsistence, a capital would be required, at the lowest estimate, of one hundred and twenty-five million dollars, or more than six times the estimated value of all the landed property in the State.

But suppose that this capital could be profitably used in cotton manufacturing, would this be the best way of applying it?

Mr. Gregg says that three fourths of the eight hundred adults whom he has collected at Graniteville are not able to read or to write their names.

"With the aid of ministers of the gospel on the spot to preach to them and lecture them on the subject, we have obtained but about sixty children for our school, of about a hundred which are in the place.   We are satisfied that nothing but time and patience will enable us to bring them all out.   *   *   *   Notwithstanding our rule that no one can be permitted to occupy our houses who does not send all his children to school that are between the ages of six and twelve, it was with some difficulty, at first, that we could make up even a small school." [1]

Mr. Taylor, a co-laborer of Mr. Gregg, says :

"The question has often been asked, Will Southern operatives equal Northern in their ability to accomplish factory work ? As a general answer, I would reply in the affirmative ; but at the

---

[1] Address to South Carolina Institute.

same time it may with justice be said they cannot at present, even in our best factories, accomplish as much as is usual in Northern mills. The habitude of our people has been to anything but close application to manual labor, and it requires time to bring the whole habits of a person into a new train." [1]

As affording an argument against establishing factories in towns, Mr. Gregg refers to the history of manufacturing in Augusta. I myself had a singular confirmation of the correctness of his views in this respect in the information given me by the landlord of a hotel in Augusta, who said, in answer to my inquiries, that the hands employed in the factories were country people who had been induced by a promise of fixed cash wages to move into town, but who were so lazy that only an immediate necessity to keep them from starvation would induce them to work. The president or foreman of the mills had been to him and implored him never to give them food when they came begging for it, as he had sometimes done, because it increased the difficulty of making them work. "If you ride past the factory," he added, "you will see them loafing about, and I reckon you never saw a meaner looking set of people anywhere. If they were niggers, they would not sell for five hundred dollars a head."

Of one of the manufacturing villages of Georgia, Tobler's Creek, the Rev. Mr. White says:[2]

"The character of the operatives is marked by the usual traits which distinguish the poor uneducated class of this country. Of the whole population of the village, which amounts to two hundred and forty, there are not twenty who can either read

---

[1] De Bow's *Review*, January, 1850.

[2] *Statistics*, p. 575

or write. * * * Nearly all the families residing here are those
who have been driven by necessity to engage their children to
work in the mills, whose toil on some worn out or barren piece
of land was not sufficient to supply their wants."

Yet the same authority says elsewhere, [1] " No
one can visit this section of the country without forming a favorable opinion of the character
of its population, the greater part are snug farmers,
out of debt."

I have previously shown that the population from
which Mr. Gregg's operatives are drawn is a rather
superior one to that of other parts of the State.

Is it not obvious that the capital required to have
the slightest remedial effect would be much better
employed in transferring the raw cotton to a free country and there manufacturing it, or that it would be far
more economical to transport, en masse, a body of
decent, intelligent, disciplined, and industrious work-
people to South Carolina, than to enlist, drill, and
educate to the necessary degree of intelligence for effective operatives, the wretched starvelings and wild men
of the pine woods, who have grown up under the
educational influence of slavery? It may be replied
that the labor of these latter may be procured at half
the price per day of the more intelligent and industrious
class. But how long would they be content with these
low wages after they had become sufficiently intelligent
to earn them? Knowing that, on free soil, as it would
be impossible long to prevent their knowing, the same
degree of intelligence and the same amount of labor
would earn twice the amount of comfort, how long

[1] *Statistics*, p. 576

would it be before Mr. Gregg's "communities" would take themselves to free soil, or—make free soil of South Carolina? It will help us to an answer to look for an instant at Missouri.

In 1849, in Missouri, only fourteen counties out of one hundred were returned as sending above twenty per cent. of their whole population to school. Seven years afterwards came the presidential election, and the next year a State election, hotly canvassed, in which the representative of the administration party declared the question between himself and his opponent to be between the fortification of slavery and emancipation. His opponent courageously accepted it, and was denounced by that name so odious to ignorant Southern citizens, abolitionist. What did the administration party gain by it in those counties where education had been least obstructed? In six of these counties but three hundred and twenty-eight votes, while in eight of these counties the vote against it was increased over that of the presidential election fourteen hundred and forty-six votes.

It is, however, as impracticable, as it would be unsafe to the present system, to introduce white operatives in large numbers from free soil. Impracticable, because, except at greatly enhanced wages, they will not endure the necessary discomfort of the life of working people in a Slave State; unsafe, because, with their intelligence, the antagonism of slavery to their interests could not be concealed from them. They are naturally, in the words of a South Carolina editor

before quoted, "enemies to the peculiar institution," or, as De Bow says, " European [or intelligent, in contradistinction to African or ignorant] labor * * * has not taken foothold in our limits, evidencing thus an incapacity to adapt itself to our condition." It is from the admission of German laborers into Missouri that the agitation for emancipation in that State has arisen. The Southern gentlemen could not occupy the land with their forces, not even with a single slave family to a square mile in many parts. They could not afford to "take up" or hold all they left unoccupied and have not the slightest production from it. Much as the Germans disliked the proximity of slaves, they could not resist the temptation to buy this rich unoccupied land at a fourth part of the value of similar soil in the adjoining Free States; government could not refuse to sell it them, and so came the catastrophe of popular education and of discussion of the value of slavery right in the midst of a slave-holding State.

How can such a process be prevented from going on, or from recurring?

The Charleston *Mercury* says:

" Travelling in any direction, broad uncultivated lands and beds of mineral wealth, still unopened, lie before you. Settlement and cultivation mark only the most fertile spots. In South Carolina, one of the oldest States, thousands upon thousands of acres of surpassing richness stretch along her rivers, crowned with the unshorn forest. * * * These remarks have a much stronger application to the newer States of the South. Florida, Alabama, Mississippi, Arkansas, and Texas exhibit this want of labor in far more startling degrees."

Mr. Spratt, writing from Charleston to the editor of

the New Orleans *Delta*, (September, 1859), upon the
settlement of Kansas, which the South then expected to
make a Slave State before 1860 [says]:

" Without slaves, there will be little advantage in having it
nominally a Slave State. * * * The State of Delaware is
nominally a Slave State, but it were madness to rely on Delaware for aid ; and Missouri even, which has ninety thousand
slaves, has an abolition party to contest for power.

" So circumstanced, it is to be doubted whether Kansas can ever
acquire the slaves to make her in fact a Slave State ; but should
she do so, she must take them from Maryland, Virginia, Kentucky, Tennessee, or Missouri—no one of which has slaves
enough now to sustain the perfect integrity of a slave system.
Maryland reels upon the line between slavery and the isms, and
cast her vote for Fillmore in the late election.   Virginia is
threatened with a colony of New Englanders to cultivate a space
she cannot cover with slave labor.

" In Kentucky it has been proposed to manumit the slaves.
Tennessee is aghast at the mention of the slave trade, and
Missouri, as I have said, has an abolition party to contest for
power.   It can never strengthen slavery to take slaves from those
States to Kansas, and perhaps there is no place in the Union
where one hundred thousand slaves could be so profitably
planted as upon the soil of the brave old State of Virginia."

Thus, while we are every year presented with new
projects from Southern politicians for an increase of territory, are called upon to further stimulate the expand-
ing and dispersing tendency, some answer must be given
at home to the question, What are we going to do
with it?

" While we have millions of acres open to slave occupation,
yet a perfect wilderness, while some of the longest settled parts
of our present territory are every year regaining more and
more of their original wilderness condition, from the dispersion
of our labor over new wildernesses, when it is certain that civi-

lized laborers will not come upon our territory, or that if they do they will wrest it from us, what can we do with more territory? What can we do with what we have?

Mr. De Bow says :

"To one who has observed the signs of the times, the evidence is irresistible, that the question of labor supply is at this moment attracting in every part of the South and of the Southwest a degree of attention which has never been accorded to it before, stimulated as the question is by the almost boundless and now but partially occupied domain in our possession *or within our reach*, adapted to rich and productive cultivation ; by the increasing demand and enhanced prices obtained for every description of product peculiar to that domain, and by the unprecedented rise in the value of the only species of labor which it is capable of employing." [1]

It will profit us to observe how the South, becoming, in these last few years, gradually aware of the dilemma into which its policy of extension has carried it, goes to work to relieve itself.   Up to this time it is only at a few points, in the vicinity of commercial centres, where the contact of men with each other is most frequent, that the dread of entering upon any discussion is not the strongest feeling manifested.   The more impetuous only as yet have propounded a remedy, and this they advocate not earnestly but frantically ; thus :

FROM THE CHARLESTON "MURCURY"

" The alternative to the South is, whether she will continue to depend solely upon the natural increase of her slaves, for development and colonization, wholly inadequate as it is for either, or, despising for once and for ever the whinings of fanaticism,

---

[1] Letter to W. L. Yancey, published generally in Southern newspapers, July, 1859.

she will brush from her path its flimsy obstacles, and demand
that the original and true source of her labor shall be no longer
closed—that Africa and America shall be free to reciprocate
blessings? If, when slavery was deemed an evil, Southern men
consented to the abolition of the slave trade, as the precursor of
emancipation, will they adhere to the same policy when slavery
is proved to be a blessing—nay, the very heart blood of the
South? Are they still advocates of emancipation? Do they not
perceive that by such a course they are preparing the way of
abolition? It is worthy of a free people to consent to absolute
restrictions upon their legitimate progress, when progress is to
them, more than to all others, the very necessity of their existence? Shall the North be permitted to supply her demand for
labor, wherewith to usurp the common territories, and abolition-
ize the government by an emigration, attended with all the horrors of the slave trade, while the South is tied hand and foot?
Will she perpetuate a policy which stigmatizes her civilization,
betrays her cause into the silliest inconsistencies, and tends
to her complete annihilation? Will she permit her vast and
splendid resources to be wasted, because fanaticism and political rivalry demand the sacrifice?"

FROM THE SAME

"If it benefits the African, and benefits the Southern planter,
and benefits the trader who brings over the slaves, who is there
to be injured by it? We are to be content with the answer that
there is a pack of fools and Pharisees in England and the
Northern States, whose feelings are hurt by the horrors of the
slave trade, and that the general assembly of French philoso-
phers have decided that a man can rightfully have no property
in man."

FROM THE CHARLESTON "STANDARD"

"It is first necessary to see that we are right, to look at this
great question of the slave trade, and see if, in fact, we require
its establishment, and, if so, we will demand its re-establishment within the Union, or we will re-establish it to ourselves."

FROM THE "STATES RIGHT LOUISIANIAN"

"Unless the slave trade be re-established, slavery, instead of

increasing, must necessarily diminish its borders, and, after a certain length of time, be extinguished. Slaveholders, for the present, have no other interest than to strengthen and defend it in all places where it already exists, and where it is an essential and integrant part of the domestic institutions."

We cannot people a country with blacks or whites, without a *people* to do it with, and the simple truth is, the South has not the black labor to spare for any such an enterprise.

"We cannot hold our own in such a race until we increase the slave population, and that can only be done with effective rapidity by transferring them from the great hive of barbarian slavery in Africa to the scene of humanized and Christianized slavery in America. If the South desires to maintain the conflict, so far against her in its results, for an equality of rights in the territories, and for the preservation of an equilibrium of political power in the Union, we know of no other way to do it but to go to work at once in an effort to repeal the laws of the Union which prohibit the African slave trade. This is a powerful, active, and vital issue ; and pushed to the wall by her fanatical enemies, we see no course open to the South but to strip it of all meretricious surroundings of prejudice and cant, and to discuss and meet it boldly on its merits."

For heaven's sake, do not propose anything so startling, is the first reply ; for the discussion which it must provoke will be ruinous to us.

And to this time, therefore, the advocates of the slave trade are chiefly engaged in arguing, not the feasibility of their scheme, but the safety of arguing its feasibility. Mr. De Bow, for one, believes "it is an idle assumption that the discussion will divide and distract the South. The division, at most," he contends, " will prove to be of no more importance than such as already exists in regard to cardinal matters of State

and federal policy ; (in saying which he can only refer
to the naturalization question, which has been the base
of the only party divisions of the South in the last six
years) ; "and which," continues Mr. De Bow, " is at
any moment ready to be sacrified when the common
interest is menaced. We must trust our fellow-citizens thus far, and they in return will suspect us [who ?]
neither of distrust or of treason."[1]

It is clear that the majority are, at the opening,
against the African party, that is to say, are against
discussion, but it is equally clear that the African party
cannot be silenced, and that a practical agreement
will be arrived at, is in many parts already arrived at,
as follows :

The question shall be argued, and the South given
over to discussion, upon these conditions : That it shall
always be taken for granted on both sides—First, that
free society is full of morbid and dangerous elements,
not respectable, irreligious, and altogether offensive to
a true Southerner. Second, that slavery, under our
present laws is a Bible institution, and the most effective agent of freedom, Christianity, Democracy, civilization, and wealth. Third, that any man who proposes
measures which involve an amelioration of the condition of the slaves, or which look in the slightest toward
the possibility of any portion of them or of their
descendants being allowed to take care of themselves,
shall be called an abolitionist, and as such shall be

[1] Letter to Hon. Wm. L. Yancey.

publicly entertained. Fourth, that the man who shows the greatest regard for slavery is the truest Democrat and truest Christian, and shall be held to deserve best of his country.

Wherever the main question is yet at all discussed, these conditions are rigidly adhered to. South of Washington, not a single newspaper article, not a single pamphlet, not a single sermon or address has been published, since the scheme was suggested, in which these conditions have been in the slightest degree infringed.

The opponents of importation may manage to postpone a general engagement upon the final issue, but it is impossible that it shall be no more than postponed, and when they can no longer avoid it, they will have to fight on ground upon which the African party will be irresistible.

For who can object to this scheme, and on what grounds can he object to it, that will not, as soon as the battle is at all hot, stamp him an enemy to the South, a traitor, an infidel? Immorality? It would not be well for a man to suggest that line of argument. "Either slavery is right or it is wrong, and it is a greater and more unmitigated wrong in him who keeps the negro to that sad condition than in him who originally fastened the yoke upon him." Thus replies in advance the Charleston *Standard*, and who dare rejoin with the Charleston mob, to maintain the fundamental conditions of the discussion, before him?

The only resistance to be feared at the South is from

those ignorant citizens whose ruling passion is hatred
not of slavery, but of negroes, and who with some
difficulty are now restrained from demanding measures
which will deport them all from their own vicinity.
Nevertheless, they can be managed. Assure them that
an importation of the original savage stock is a measure
directed against those who would like to give the
negroes who have come of families two hundred years
under American training a chance to better themselves
when they can, without fighting or breaking laws, and
they will yield their prejudices.

Is evidence needed of how the plan carries, by its
mere statement, conviction to those who give it a hearing, it is found in confessions like the following,[1] the
writer of which opens his letter with expressions of
doubt. The measure is a little too startling—impracticable—he fears; but he presently adds:

"I can go thus far with you, however. I have some two
thousand acres of land that will now sell for about six dollars
an acre, and which, when twenty or even ten thousand slaves
are brought into the country from Africa, or any other quarter,
will sell for thirty dollars an acre. I think I could find it in
my breast to pocket the difference of forty-eight thousand dollars, and trust to casuists to determine whether I came honestly
by it. I am not sure but I could go a little further. I have an
interest in a gold mine, whose work requires no very great intelligence, and which yields from two to four dollars a day to
the hand. I am now purchasing negroes at from eight hundred
to eleven hundred dollars each. If I could have an opportunity
of purchasing some one or two thousand at about two hundred
dollars each, I am not certain that I should insist upon their

---

Published in the Charleston *Standard*.

having been torn from their families either in this or the adjoining States, but could even find it in my heart to take them with a knowledge of the fact that they had come from Africa. We want labor, and only labor, to a most rapid and astonishing development of wealth, but our sources of supply are limited. What we get is limited. What we get is taken from some other employments in our own vicinity. The gain at one point is to be diminished by the loss at another, and there is no other way of it but that we must set to work and laboriously breed the labor by which the golden harvest of our country is to be ultimately gathered."

Another, writing to the same editor from the State Capitol of South Carolina, says:

"There are many gentlemen of character and standing in the State who daily tell me that they are not ashamed of slavery [the man would be a hero, indeed, who dare speak otherwise in that locality, but what follows?], *or the means by which it was established*. They confess the want of labor to every interest in the country, and express the assurance that the only kind of labor we are capable of receiving, without a disturbance of existing relations, is in the form of slavery."

The domestic slave trade, slave auctions, the forcible separation of husbands and wives, of parents and children; the compulsion to adultery of members of Christian churches, without legal remedy; and a commerce (the internal slave trade) once characterized by John Randolph, of Roanoke, on the floor of Congress, as "the infernal traffic," has been maintained by convincing men who objected to it, on the score of morality and humanity, of its necessity for the "safety" of the South, that is (as assumed by those interested) of the political equality in power of the slave-holding minority with the non-slave-holding majority of the

republic.[1] It cannot be doubted that the African slave
trade is, at this time, a much more obvious and immediately pressing necessity for that purpose than the
domestic slave trade has ever been.   And the moral

---

[1] It is an infamous libel which we by our partisanship have
fastened upon ourselves, that the North has an aggressive
spirit towards the South. It has always been directly otherwise. Mr. Webster, in his plea for the compromise on the 7th
of March, 1850, said these true words :

"The honorable member from South Carolina [Mr. Calhoun]
observed there has been a majority all along in favor of the
North. If that be true, sir, the North has acted either very
liberally and kindly, or very weakly; for they never exercised
that majority efficiently five times in the history of this government, when a division or trial of strength arose. Never.
Whether they were out-generalled, or whether it was owing to
other causes, I shall not stop to consider ; but no man acquainted with the history of the Union can deny that the
general lead in the politics of the country, for three fourths of
the period that has elapsed since the adoption of the
Constitution, has been a Southern lead."

The Charleston *Courier*, commenting on a discourse delivered
in South Carolina, against the immediate secession of that great
Power from our Union, to which the *Courier* itself is yet kindly
opposed, says it "truthfully as well as strongly details and de-
picts the various occasions on which Southern interests have
obtained the mastery in Congress, or, at least, important advantages, which are well worthy of the consideration of all who
erroneously suppose that the action of the general government
has been, on the whole, adverse to slavery. The truth is that
our government, although hostile in its incipiency [that is,
until after the administration of Jefferson] to domestic slavery,
and starting into political being with a strong bent toward
abolition, yet afterwards so changed its policy that its action
for the most part, and with only a few exceptions, has fostered
the slave-holding interest, and swelled it from six to fifteen
States, and from a feeble and sparse population to one of ten
millions."

objections to it are to be more easily overcome. As, therefore, a South Carolinian quoted elsewhere says,[1] "*If men are to make a fuss about it, they will have to begin with the internal slave trade.*"

After all, then, the difficulty is at the North; the North can never be convinced or brought to consent to the reopening of the foreign slave trade.

Why not?

Evidently there would be no difficulty, if the same conditions of discussion could be imposed at the North —even in parts of the North. There are spots where this might be hoped for. If a party at the North could be got to accept those conditions of discussion—could be got to take ground that slavery must be considered a good thing for low people, or for niggers alone, and could be kept in ascendency in a few States, or a few parts of States, that would be sufficient; the South being united to control Congress and the navy, and remove the present difficulties.[2]

[1] *Seaboard Slave States*, vol. ii, p. 161.

[2] "We took occasion to notice, a few days since the resolution reported by Mr. Slidell, from the Committee on Foreign Relations, proposing to give to England and France notice of the abrogation of the treaty stipulations by which we are bound to keep a naval force upon the African coast for the suppression of the slave trade. We stated then our approbation of this measure, from the conviction that it is onerous to our country, destructive to our seamen engaged in this service, and utterly inefficient for the purpose intended. We also approve of it for another reason, which we will state with perfect frankness to the people of this country. We have no sympathy in the purposes of this convention, and no wish for its success."— Charleston *Standard*.

Not to directly and avowedly legalize the traffic ; that would be too much to hope of this generation. The friends of the institution at the North could hardly be asked to advocate that.   It would be too much for the South to demand that, except to make a less advanced position appear more tenable—except to prepare the way for a new "compromise."   But the friends of slavery at the North can be brought to adopt measures in the interest of the South, which, if carried, will soon involve the African slave trade as a necessity—a necessity of that kind which knows no law, which cares for no law, which will evade or overcome all law and all legal force that seeks to prevent the profits which would soon attend the supply of labor to the insatiable demand of capitalists for the South.

"The course we propose to pursue is this : Let each Southern State say, through her legislature, that the importation—immigration if you prefer—of the African race to the South, is the means appointed of heaven for their civilization, and that as their coming will be mutually beneficial both to us and to them, hereafter it shall be lawful for all ships having such *passengers* on board, freely to land them at any port or harbor in the State ; that the sheriff of the district in which the port may be situated shall lodge such passengers at the expense of the State, until they can find employment, and shall moreover pay to the captain of the ship bringing them liberal passage money to be charged against the State in the first instance, and pro vided for in any subsequent contract respecting their service and employment."

Governor Moore, of Alabama, being a candidate for re-election, and addressed on the subject of the slave trade, says that "he is in favor of *modifying* the laws which make it piracy, and discriminating among the

¹ *Pee Dee Times.*

different grades of the offense, but thinks that neither this nor any other question should be allowed to divide the South in the crisis of the approaching presidential campaign.''

This indicates the policy of the mischief-makers. Insist that it is a mistake to suppose that slavery is an evil, and wait for a chance to demand, with some show of force, as a matter of courtesy and of safety to the Union, the modification of the laws against the African slave trade.   Then the Cuba game.

The Florida jury, which lately had a slaver captain in their hands, published a card in which they pledged themselves to labor unremittingly for a ''repeal of all laws which directly or indirectly condemn'' the institution of slavery, or ''those who have inherited or maintained it.'' They denominated the prejudice which has existed against the business of importing Africans ''a sickly sentiment of pretended philanthropy.''

Undoubtedly the African slave trade is yet protested against by many. It would be unjust and unkind to say that the leading politicians of the South had adopted it, and were only restrained from openly advocating it from a fear that by so doing they would open ground upon which a conservative party could rally.

It is not unjust to say ; it is certainly true that there is a necessity upon the South—a pressing necessity—a necessity of constantly increasing pressure, which, if not in some other way met, must inevitably lead to the renewed importation of Africans.

Says a Virginian, addressing Elihu Burritt :

" Europe needs it ; every steamer brings us intelligence that efforts are to be made to produce more cotton.   Tropical and semi-tropical products—some of them articles of prime necessity—are constantly increasing in price.   Already sugar is so high that its consumption in Europe is becoming a luxury. Cotton is rising daily ; and no sugar or cotton lands are brought into cultivation.   Nor can they.   There is a want of labor to cultivate these lands.   Give us more of the only kind of labor that will enable us to keep up the supply of the raw material, and the free labor of Europe and the North can find employment, and consequently bread in its manufacture.   Diminish the supply of cotton, or let it not increase to keep pace with the demand, and you throw thousands out of employment, and bring starvation upon all manufacturing communities.

" America needs it.   The North needs it, as Western Europe does, for clothing, to furnish the raw material for manufacture. The South needs it to bring more land into cultivation."

This is the plain truth, and there is no avoiding it. The African slave trade may easily be made a more pressing necessity than it is at present by an enlargement of the field of slave occupation ; but it is already, to-day, a necessity more urgent than the Dred Scott decision was yesterday, than the repeal of the Missouri Compromise was the day before yesterday, than the Fugitive Slave Law was the day before that ; a necessity more imperative and obvious than the internal slave trade ever has been ; a necessity less sincerely resisted, and by far less logically, less convincingly, by the politicians of the South to-day, than the inter-State slave trade was by those of the last generation.[1]

[1] " Both South Carolina and Georgia have at different times passed acts to prevent the internal slave trade.   Governor Williams, of South Carolina, in his annual message to the Legisla-

For the politicians of the South it is a necessity which can no more be avoided than agitation can be avoided by those of the North. As, says Mr. Spratt, in concluding the article on the settlement of Kansas, from which I recently quoted : "The foreign slave trade is the certain road to power [with the three fifths rule] for the South, and the *only road to power* within the Union." [1]

Is dissolution or the slave trade to be the next alternative presented us by the politicians of the South ?

I see not how any man in his senses, comprehensively viewing the whole ground, can escape from the conclusion, that, if not the next, it is but a few steps beyond it.

Is there no ground on which a Union party can permanently stand in the South ?

There is.

" Slavery shall, by general consent, be hereafter confined within its present limits."

There is no other.

Is this ruin to the South ?

---

ture of that State (1817) spoke of it as a 'remorseless and merciless traffic, a ceaseless dragging along the highways of a crowd of suffering beings to minister to insatiable avarice, condemned alike by enlightened humanity, wise policy, and the prayers of the just.' "—Hildreth, vol. vi., p. 614.

[1] "It may be said that the slave trade can never be re-established within this Union. This may be true, perhaps, and we would regret the alternative thus presented to us. We have, with the Northern States, a common independence, a common government and a common history, and we would regret the necessity for a separation ; but if we have a separate existence to

Ruin to the present ruling politicians of the South, it perhaps is.

WHAT MIGHT BE ANTICIPATED FROM A TERRITORIAL RESTRICTION OF SLAVERY

The necessity of the South really demands only cheaper labor and cheaper means of exchanging results of labor. To restrict the region within which slave labor may be employed, would, after the varying demands for labor of different parts within the region had been equalized, check the further emigration of slaves from any particular district. As the natural increase of negroes would then in great measure remain where it was born, any given district would soon be better supplied than at present with laborers. (This tendency might be increased by legal restrictions on the transfer, or State exportation of slaves.) With a better provision of laborers, land would increase in production. With an increased production of each district, new facilities of transportation to the consumer would be required from that district. With a diminished cost of labor, these facilities could be more cheaply obtained ; with a larger amount to carry, more effective

defend, we must have the means by which we are to defend it ; if we have war within this Union for the preservation of our institutions, we must have within this Union the right to use our own natural implements of warfare, or we must leave it. It is first necessary to see that we are right, to look at this great question of the slave trade, and see if, in fact, we require its re-establishment and if so, we will demand its re-establishment within this Union, or we will re-establish it to ourselves."— Charleston *Standard.*

means of carriage could be provided with profit. With the cost of exportation, the cost of importation would be lessened. Articles of use, comfort, and luxury, including tools and machinery, and the results of study in improved methods of agriculture, and in all industry, would be made more accessible, cheaper, and more common. This would act further, and constantly further and further, to lessen the cost of the labor necessary to obtain a given value of cotton or of any other production of the soil.

The present facility of acquiring land in the cotton States, the capital needed for its purchase not exceeding, for fresh soil, on an average, three dollars an acre, and the large outlay of capital needed to obtain labor, necessarily induces that mode of agriculture which has desolated so large a portion of the seaboard Slave States. Twenty slave laborers cost over twenty thousand dollars.[1] They will cultivate four hundred acres of land, which costs less than a tenth of that sum. Knowing that he can buy as much more as he wants, at an equally low rate, why, when the production of his land decreases, should the slave owner drain it, or manure it, or, "rest" it, or vary his crops, to prevent further ex-

[1] The following paragraph, from a North Carolina newspaper, gives the latest quotations:

"We learn, through a friend, that on Monday last the following property was sold in Salisbury at the prices annexed: Leve, $1,600; George, $1,895; Charlotte and two children, $1,600; Henry, $1,476; Alick, $1,600; and Hiram, $2,130. The above prices show that negro property is not depreciating in value."

haustion? It will cost twenty dollars' worth of labor to manure an acre. Why make this expenditure when he can obtain other land at five dollars an acre (fenced and ready for the plough), which, without manure, will return just as much cotton for the same amount of labor (in cultivation merely) as this with it? Why, when on fresh soil he can get three hundred dollars' worth of cotton a year for each slave employed in cultivating it, should he apply that labor to some other crop on his old land which would return him not more than a hundred dollars for each slave employed? Why, in these circumstances, should he arrange to remain half his life on the same spot? and if he is not expecting to remain, why should he expend his costly labor on houses and roads and bridges and fruit trees, or on schools and churches, or on railroads and wharves? Fifteen years hence his land will no longer be worth cultivating for cotton, and it will then afford no business to a railroad or a steamboat, and in the meantime the difference between wagoning and railing or boating his cotton to the merchant would do but little toward defraying the cost of a railroad or establishing a steamboat route.

" In 1825, Madison County [Alabama], cast 3,000 votes; now [1855], it cannot cast exceeding 2,500. * * * The freshness of its agricultural glory is gone; the vigor of its youth is extinct, and the spirit of desolation seems brooding over it." These are what the Hon. C. C. Clay, member of Congress from Alabama, describes as " memorials of the artless and exhausting culture of cotton " in the State he represents. But why

thus artless and exhausting? He himself gives the answer : "Our small planters, after taking the cream off their lands, * * * are going further West and South, in search of other virgin lands, which they will despoil and impoverish in a similar manner." And when they have done this, they fully anticipate going still further and further, and again and again repeating the process. Can the men who do this and who have these anticipations be expected to build railroads, or bridges, or schools, or churches? Can they, wanting nothing but corn, coffee, hogs, niggers, and camp furniture, support mechanics or merchants? Can they form by themselves a prosperous or respectable community? Will the annexation of Sonora, of the whole of Mexico, Nicaraugua, Cuba, and the Amazon region enable them to do so? Except the African slave trade is re-established, it will have—and every Southern gentleman knows it and will acknowledge it—directly the contrary influence. The first thing necessary to the prosperity of the South is, to make possible to its citizens the comforts of civilized life. To this is first essential the civilized idea of home; and this will not be gained while the nomadic and vagabond propensities of its petty patriarchs continue to be stimulated by our government as they have been hitherto.

OBJECTIONS

Practically, I have heard but one urged : that the danger of insurrection would increase. This supposes that a portion of the non-slave-holding population

would remove to free territory, or at least that the slave population would increase more rapidly than the free.

I believe that the counteracting element would soon be obvious, in the incoming of a "town population" of whites, which would follow from the greater abundance of raw material—the production of unskilled labor—and the better markets which an increasing density even of a plantation population would occasion. This could be insured, if thought necessary, by laws, for a time, prohibiting slave labor to be employed for any other purpose than the production of raw materials and in domestic duties, thus obliging planters to give employment to free, instead of using, as at present, slave mechanics.

No one apprehends that a plan of general insurrection will be devised and successfully executed by negroes over a large extent of country. The danger is that the slaves will rise and make a temporarily successful stand in some of those districts in which the proportion of white inhabitants is the smallest (it being now one man to a hundred slaves of both sexes, in some parts), and that from such a success an insurrectionary contagion will be communicated to adjoining districts, in which the strength of the whites is otherwise sufficient to leave no room for apprehension.

There is now a law in several of the Slave States, perhaps in all, which requires that there shall be at least one white man resident on every plantation. This law, while it recognizes the principle that each owner of slaves should be required to maintain any arrangement

that is deemed necessary by the legislature for the safe
control of his property, is very inadequate to its purpose,
for precisely under the circumstances where danger is
most to be apprehended, it posts the weakest guard.   I
have seen four adjoining plantations, the aggregate
slave population of which was close upon one thousand,
with but one overseer living on each, and these, together
with one other, the only white men within several hours'
ride ; all the land in the vicinity being, in fact, engrossed in these great plantations.   In a region of small
plantations there are not only more whites on the
plantations themselves, proportionately to the number
of blacks, but almost always resident, some families of
non-slave-holding whites.

Suppose that, instead of this inefficient law, it should
be enacted that each owner of a plantation on which
lived twenty-five slaves, should either himself reside,
or should cause a white overseer to reside on each such
plantation, and that for every twenty-five slaves, additional to the first twenty-five, he should cause another
white man, as overseer or assistant overseer, to reside.
Further : that each such owner or overseer (one only
for each plantation, however large), should be held
responsible to the magistrates of the county for the pru-
dent guardianship of the said slaves ; that he should be
required to report at stated intervals the number he had
in charge, and any other particulars necessary to give
confidence that a sufficient guard was maintained.   It
would not be necessary that the assistants should be
employed as overseers.   They might be mechanics; they

might be any poor whites already resident in the vicinity, who could be depended upon to be always within reach if wanted by the responsible overseer.

Such a law would not only be far more effective than the present one, for the present circumstances, it would be equally so for a slave population of ten times the present average density ; because even though the white population should not increase proportionately, those classes of it which are now mainly relied upon to prevent insurrection, would be stronger, and more effectively stationed for the purpose.[1]

It is, however, the opinion of students on the subject whose judgment is most respected at the South, that the slave population, if densely settled, would be less dangerous and more efficiently managed than as at present, even without any such precaution as I have suggested, and this opinion seems reasonable. The following is from a *Memoir on Negro Slavery*, written by Chancellor Harper, of South Carolina, edited by Mr. De Bow, of Louisiana, in which state it was published not ten years ago, while it is yet exposed for sale by booksellers in Mobile and Charleston, without causing

---

[1] If to such a law there should be added a provision requiring that no one should be deemed an overseer, within the meaning of the act, who had not been certified by specified authories to be a man of good character and of adequate intelligence and information for the legal duties to be imposed upon him, it would not only be a humane act toward the slaves, but would practically embody a well-distributed and trustworthy police force, vastly better for its purpose, and costing the community less than the present rural patrols.

their expulsion.   Hence it may be inferred that the
mob as yet really hold the same opinions :

" President Dew " (whose writings have also escaped being
placed on the Index Expurgatorius)," President Dew," says
Chancellor Harper, endorsed as to safety by Commissioner De
Bow, "has very fully shown how utterly vain are the fears of
those who, though there may be no danger for the present, yet
apprehend great danger for the future, when the number of
slaves shall be greatly increased.   He has shown that the larger
and more condensed society becomes, the easier it will be to
maintain subordination, supposing the relative numbers of the
different classes to remain the same, or even if there should be
a very disproportionate increase of the enslaved class."

   *   *   *   *   *   *   *   *

" When the demand for agricultural labor shall be fully supplied, then of course the labor of slaves will be directed to other
employments and enterprises.   Already it begins to be found
that, in some instances, it may be used as profitably in works
of public improvement.   As it becomes cheaper, it will be
applied to more various purposes, and combined in larger
masses.   It may be commanded and combined with more
facility than any other sort of labor, and the laborer, kept in
strict subordination, will be less dangerous to the security of
society than in any other country which is crowded and overstocked with a class of what are called free laborers.   Let it be
remembered that all the great and enduring monuments of
human art and industry—the wonders of Egypt, the everlasting
works of Rome, were created by the labor of slaves." [1]

But the Egyptians and the Romans enjoyed the
advantage of an unimpeded importation of slaves,
when engaged in these works.   It was a *dense*
slave population only which made them possible;
and if the South is to rival them it must reopen
the African slave trade, or put a check upon the dis-

[1] *Resources*, vol. ii., p. 233.

persion of its laborers, which is thus shown to be as much a measure of safety as of glory.

The alleged danger, on which is based the plea of the necessity of the South to extend slavery, I propose to yet further consider in the last chapter. I will now simply add that the advantages and the safety of a restriction of the territorial field of slave labor, and of other measures which, as I have suggested, might be employed for the same purposes, will be found much more fully and clearly set forth in any of the many able papers which have been published in South Carolina since the last presidential election in advocacy of the African slave trade.

CHAPTER IX

CHARACTER AND MANNERS

FORMULA FOR JUSTIFYING SLAVERY

SINCE the growth of the cotton demand has doubled the value of slave labor, and with it the pecuniary inducement to prevent negroes from taking care of themselves, hypotheses and easy methods for justifying their continued slavery have been multiplied. I have not often conversed with the planter about the condition of the slaves, that he did not soon make it evident, that a number of these were on service in his own mind, naïvely falling back from one to another, if a few inquiries about matters of fact were addressed him without obvious argumentative purpose. The beneficence of slavery is commonly urged by an exposition not only of the diet, and the dwellings, and the jollity, and the devotional eloquence of the negroes, but also by demonstrations of the high mental attainments to which individuals are already found to be arriving. Thus there is always at hand some negro mathematician, who is not merely held to be far in advance of the native Africans, but who beats most white men in his quickness and accuracy in calculation, and who is at the same time considered to be so thoroughly trust-

154

worthy, that he is constantly employed by his master as an accountant and collecting agent; or some negro whose reputation for ingenuity and skill in the management and repair of engines, sugar-mills, cotton presses, or other machinery, is so well established that his services are more highly valued, throughout a considerable district, than any white man's; or some negro who really manages his owner's plantation, his agricultural judgment being deferred to as superior to that of any overseer or planter in the county. Scarcely a plantation did I visit on which some such representative black man was not acknowledged and made a matter of boasting by the owner, who, calling attention perhaps to the expression of intelligence and mien of self-confidence which distinguished his premium specimen, would cheerfully give me a history of the known special circumstances, practically constituting a special mental feeding, by which the phenomenon was to be explained. Yet it might happen that the same planter would presently ask, pointing to the brute-like countenance of a moping field hand, what good would freedom be to such a creature? And this would be one who had been provided from childhood with food, and shelter, and clothing with as little consideration of his own therefor as for the air he breathed; who had not been allowed to determine for himself with whom he should associate; with what tools and to what purpose he should labor; who had had no care on account of his children; who had no need to provide for old age; who had never had need to count five-and-twenty; the

highest demand upon whose faculties had been to discriminate between cotton and crop-grass, and to strike one with a hoe without hitting the other; to whose intelligence, though living in a civilized land, the pen and the press, the mail and the telegraph, had contributed nothing; who had no schooling as a boy; no higher duty as a man than to pick a given quantity of cotton between dawn and dark; and of whom, under this training and these confinements, it might well be wondered that he was found able to understand and to speak the language of human intelligence any more than a horse.

Again, one would assure me that he had witnessed in his own time an obvious advance in the quality of the slaves generally ; they were more active, less stupid, employed a larger and more exact vocabulary, and were less superstitious, obstinate, and perverse in their habits of mind than when he was himself a boy ; but I had only to presume that, with this rapid improvement, the negroes would soon be safely allowed to take some step toward freedom, to be assured with much more apparent confidence than before, that in the special quality which originally made the negro a slave, there had been no gain ; that indeed it was constantly becoming more evident that he was naturally too deficient in forecasting capacity to be able to learn how to take civilized care of himself.

As a rule, when the beneficence of slavery is argued by Southerners, an advancing intellectual as well as moral condition of the mass of negroes is assumed, and the high

attainments of individuals are pointed to as evidence of
what is to be expected of the mass, if the system is not
disturbed. Suggest that any modification of the system
would enlarge its beneficence, however, and an exception to the general rule, as regards the single quality of
providence, is at once alleged, and in such a manner,
that one cannot but get the impression that, in this
quality, the negro is believed to be retrograding as
surely as he is advancing in everything else ; and this
is one method by which the unconditional perpetuation
of the system, as it is, is justified. Such a justification
must of course involve the supposition that in the tenth
generation of an unremitted training, discipline, education, and custom in abject dependence upon a voluntary
provision by others, for every wish of which the grati-
fication is permitted, white men would be able, as a
rule, to gain in the quality of providence and capacity
for independent self-support.

As to the real state of the case, I find, in my own
observation, no reason for doubting, what must be
expected of those interested, that the general improvement of the slave is usually somewhat overrated, and
his forecasting ability underrated. Measures intended
to prevent a man from following his natural inclinations
often have the effect of stimulating those inclinations ;
and I believe that the system which is designed not
merely to relieve the negro from having any care for
himself, but, as far as practicable, to forcibly prevent him
from taking care of himself, in many particulars to
which he has more or less instinctive inclination, in-

stead of gradually suppressing his inclination, to some
extent stimulates it, so that the Southern negro of to-
day, however depraved in his desires, and however badly
instructed, is really a man of more cunning, shrewdness,
reticence, and persistence in what he does undertake for
himself than his father was.   The healthful use of these
qualities (which would constitute providence) is, however, in general, successfully opposed by slavery, and,
as far as the slave is concerned, nothing worse than this
can be said of the system.

Admitting that, in this view, slavery is not beneficent, or is no longer beneficent or can be but for a time
beneficent to the slave the present attitude of the South
still finds a mode of justification with many minds, in
the broad assertion that the negro is not of the nature of
mankind, therefore cannot be a subject of inhumanity.
This, of course, sweeps the field, if it does anything ;
thus (from the *Day-Book*) :

"The wide-spread delusion that Southern institutions are an
evil, and their extension dangerous—the notion so prevalent at
the North that there is a real antagonism, or that the system of
the South is hostile to Northern interests ; the weakened union
sentiment, and the utter debauchment, the absolute traitorism
of a portion of the Northern people, not only to the Union, but
to Democratic institutions, and to the cause of civilization on
this continent ; all these, with the minor and most innumerable
mischiefs that this mighty world-wide imposture has engendered or drags in its midst, rest upon the dogma, the single
assumption, the sole elementary foundation falsehood, that a
negro is a black man."

This bold ground is not as often taken at the South
as by desperate bidders for Southern confidence among

ourselves. I have heard Christian men, however, when
pushed for a justification of the sealing up of the printed
Bible, of the legal disregard of marriage, of giving
power to rascally traders to forcibly separate families,
and so on, refer to it as a hypothesis not at all to be
scouted under such circumstances. Yet, as they did so,
there stood behind their chairs, slaves, in whose veins
ran more Anglo-Saxon blood than of any African race's
blood, and among their other slaves, it, is probable
there were many descendants of Nubians, Moors,
Egyptians, and Indians, all interbred with white and
true negro tribes, so that it would be doubtful if there
remained one single absolutely pure negro, to which
animal alone their argument would strictly apply. If
the right or expediency of denying the means of
preparing themselves for freedom to these beings could
even be held to be coexistent with the evident prepon-
derance in them of certain qualities of form, color, etc.,
the number of those who are held unjustly or in-
expediently in the bonds of a perpetual slavery
is already quite large in the South, and is gradually but surely increasing—is increasing much
more rapidly than are their means of cultivating
habits which are necessary to be cultivated, before
the manliest child of white men is capable of enjoying
freedom.

There are but two methods of vindicating the habit
of depending on the labor of slaves for the development of wealth in the land, which appear to me, on the
face of them, entitled to be treated gravely. One of

these, assuming the beings held in slavery to be as yet
generally incompetent to take care of themselves in a
civilized manner, and dangerous to the life as well as to
the wealth of the civilized people who hold them in
slavery, argues that it is necessary for their humane
maintenance, and to prevent them from acquiring an
increase of the disposition and strength of mind and will
which has always been felt a source of danger to the
well-being of their masters, that all the present laws
for their mental repression should be rigidly maintained.
It is not to be denied, I think, that there is some
ground for this assumption.   Inasmuch as it is also argued that the same necessity requires that these beings,
and with them all these laws, should be carried on to
territory now free from them, we are called upon to
give a sober consideration to the argument which is
based upon it.   This I shall do in the last chapter.
The other method to which I refer assumes that by
having a well-defined class set apart for drudging and
servile labor, the remainder of a community may be
preserved free from the demeaning habits and traits of
character which, it is alleged, servile and menial obligations and the necessity of a constant devotion to labor
are sure to fix upon those who are subject to them.
Hence a peculiar advantage in morals and in manners
is believed to belong to the superior class of a community so divided.   I am inclined to think that
there is no method of justifying slavery, which
is more warmly cherished by those interested to
maintain it, than this.   I am sure that there is

none which planters are more ready to suggest to
their guests. [1]

No sensible man among us shuts his eyes to the ignorance, meanness, vice, and misery which accompa-
nies our general prosperity ; no class of statesmen, no
writers deny or ignore it. It is canvassed, published,
studied, struggled with, by all honest men, and this
not in our closets alone, but in our churches, our legis-
latures, our colleges, our newspapers, our families. We
are constantly urging, constantly using means for dis-
covering it and setting it forth plainly. We commission able men to make a business of bringing it to the
light, and we publish the statistics which their labors
supply as legislative documents to be circulated at the
general expense, in order that our misfortune may
be as well known and as exactly comprehended as
possible.

From much of all this, which so painfully and anx-
iously concerns us, we are told that the South is free.
We are told that what we bewail is seen at the South

[1] From an "Address on Climatology," before the Academy
of Science, by Dr. Barton, of New Orleans :—

"The institution of slavery operates by contrast and comparison ; it elevates the tone of the superior, adds to its refinement, allows more time to cultivate the mind, exalts the
standard in morals, manners, and intellectual endowments,
operates as a safety-valve for the evil disposed, leaving the upper race purer, while it really preserves from degradation, in
the scale of civilization, the inferior, which we see is their uniform destiny when left to themselves. The slaves constitute
essentially the lowest class, and society is immeasurably bene-
fited by having this class, which constitutes the offensive fun-
gus—the great cancer of civilized life—a vast burthen and

to be the result of a mistaken social system ; that the
South escapes that result by slavery.   We do not deny,
we daily acknowledge that there are mistakes in our system ; we endeavor to remedy them ; and we not unfrequently have to acknowledge that in doing so, we have
made some of our bad things worse.   Does slavery
relieve all ?   And without compensation ?   We often
find, upon a thorough review, that our expedients,
while they have for a time seemed to produce very
valuable results, have in fact corrected one evil by cre-
ating or enhancing another.   We have borrowed from
Peter to pay Paul.   In this way we find investigation
and discussion to be constantly essential to prevent errors and mistakes from being exaggerated and perse-
vered in unnecessarily.   Thus we—our honestly humane
part at least—are ever calling for facts, ever publishing,
proclaiming, discussing the facts of our evil.   It is only
those whose selfish interest is thought by themselves to
be served by negligence, who resist investigation and
publication, who avoid discussion.   Thus we come to
habitually associate much activity of discussion, much

---

expense to every community, under surveillance and control;
and not only so, but under direction as an efficient agent to
promote the general welfare and increase the wealth of the
community.   The history of the world furnishes no institution
under similar management, where so much good actually results
to the governors and the governed as this in the Southern
States of North America.

" It is by the existence of slavery, exempting so large a portion of our citizens from labor, that we have leisure for intellectual pursuits."— Governor Hammond, in *Southern Literary
Messenger.*

consideration, much publication with improvement—
often no doubt erroneously—still it is natural and ra-
tional that when we find no discussion of facts, no
publication, no consideration, where we find general
consideration and general discussion practically prevented by a forcible resistence to publication, we cannot but suspect there is something sadly needing to be
made better.   And this last we do find to be the case
at the South, and with regard to slavery.   Why, if
their system has such tangible evidence of its advantages within the personal knowledge of any citizen, do
they object to its alleged disadvantages being set forth
for consideration, and, if it should happen, discussion ?
True, we may be wrong, we may be mistaken in supposing that this, our constant publication and challenge
to discussion is a good thing.   Perhaps if we were better, we should talk less, know less of what evil remained to be gradually grown out of.   It might be
found that the constant consideration of our evil had
had a bad effect upon us.   But I have not found that
the people of the South are inclined to shut their eyes,
and close their ears, and bar their imaginations to the
same evil.   With the misery which prevails among us,
Southerners generally appear to be, indeed, more familiar than the most industrious of our home philan-
thropists.   Great as it is, it is really overestimated at
the South—overestimated in the aggregate at least—for
it is perhaps impossible to overestimate the sufferings
of individuals.   South of Virginia, an intelligent man
or woman is rarely met who does not maintain, with

the utmost apparent confidence, that the people who do the work of the North are, on the whole, harder driven, worse fed, and more destitute of comfort than are the slaves at the South, taking an average of both classes ; and this I heard assumed by gentlemen, the yearly cost of maintaining whose own slaves, according to their statement to me, would not equal the average monthly expenses of an equal number of the poorest class of laborers I have ever known at the North. I have heard it assumed by planters, who not only did not themselves enjoy, but who never imagined or aspired to a tithe of the comfort to which most journeymen mechanics whom I have known are habituated. I have heard it assumed by gentlemen, nine tenths of whose neighbors for a hundred miles around them lived in a manner which, if witnessed at the North, would have made them objects of compassion to the majority of our day-laborers.

A gentleman coming up the Mississippi, just after a recent "Southern Commercial Convention" at Memphis, says :

"For three days I have been sitting at a table three times a day opposite four of the fire-eaters. * * * It was evident that they were sincere ; for they declared to one another the belief that Providence was directing the South to recommence the importation of Africans, that she might lead the world to civilization and Christianity through its dependence upon her soil for cotton. All their conversation was consistent with this. They believed the South the center of Christianity and the hope of the world, while they had not the slightest doubt that the large majority of the people of the North were much more to be pitied than their own negroes. Exclusive of merchants,

manufacturers, lawyers, and politicians, they evidently imagined the whole population of the North to be quite similar to
the poor white population of the South.   Yet they had travelled
in the North, it appeared.   I could only conclude that their observation of Northern working men had been confined to the
Irish operatives of some half-finished Western railroad, living
in temporary shanties along the route.''

I have even found that conservative men, who
frankly acknowledged the many bad effects of slavery,
and confessed the conviction that the Northern Slave
States were ruined by it ; men who expressed admiration of Cassius Clay's course, and acknowledged no little sympathy with his views, and who spoke with more
contempt of their own fanatics than of the Abolitionists
themselves ; that such men were inclined to apologize
for slavery, and for their own course in acting politically
for its extension and perpetuation, by assuming certain
social advantages to exist where it prevailed.   '' There
is a higher tone in Southern society than at the North,''
they would say, '' which is, no doubt, due to the greater
leisure which slavery secures to us.   There is less anx-
iety for wealth, consequently more honesty.   This also
leads to the habit of more generous living and of hospitality, which is so characteristic of the South.''

I think that there is a type of character resulting in
a secondary way from slavery, of which Mr. Clay is
himself a noble example, which attracts admiration
and affection in a rare manner.   I shall explain this
secondary action of slavery by and by.   I have come to
the conclusion that whatever may be the good results
of slavery in the way I shall then describe, this so con-

stantly asserted, so generally conceded, of inducing a
" higher tone " of breeding, and especially of nourish-
ing the virtue of hospitality, is chimerical.

Some reader may at once be inclined to say that the
Southerners whom he has met are unquestionably better bred people than are common at the North, and that
they state as their experience that they do not find that
hospitality, that honesty, that guilelessness of dealing
one with another among the people of the North, to
which they are accustomed at home. It would remain
a question, whether the Southerners whom the reader
has met are of a common or an exceptional class ;
whether it is to slavery, or to some other circumstance,
they owe their breeding ; whether this other circumstance is dependent on slavery, or whether it may exist
(and, if so, whether, when it does exist, it produces the
same fruit), quite independently of slavery. It cannot
be said that there are no gentlemen and gentlewomen
of first water in free countries. A comparison, then,
must be a comparison of numbers. I shall, by and by,
offer the reader some assistance in making a comparison
of this kind. And if, as we hear, free-labor society is
still an experiment, and one of the results of that experiment is to be found in the low condition of portions
of our community, and it is by comparing this result
with the condition of the whites of the South that we
must judge of the success of the experiment ; it may
again be a question of numbers. As to experience of
hospitality, that is not a question of quantity or of
quality merely. I should wish to ask the reader's

Southern authorities, "Where and with whom has your experience been, North and South?" And if with a similar class and in similar circumstances, I should wish to ask further, "What do you mean by hospitality?"

In the previous chapter, I have shown that slavery does not prevent a condition of destitution of what at the North are deemed the ordinary comforts of civilized life, with a large part of the race supposed to be bene-fited especially by slavery; whether it secures to it the supposed advantage in morals and manners remains to be considered.

I think that the error which prevails in the South, with regard to the general condition of our working people, is much strengthened by the fact that a differ-ent standard of comfort is used by most persons at the South from that known at the North, and that used by Northern writers. People at the South are content and happy with a condition which few accept at the North unless with great complaint, or with expressions of resignation such as are the peculiar property of slaves at the South. If, reader, you had been travelling all day through a country of the highest agricultural capability, settled more than twenty years ago, and before night-fall should be advised by a considerate stranger to ride five miles farther, in order to reach the residence of Mr. Brown, because Mr. Brown, being a well-to-do man, and a right good fellow, had built an uncommonly good house, and got it well furnished, had a score of servants, and being at a distance from neighbors, was always glad

to entertain a respectable stranger—after hearing this, as you continued your ride somewhat impatiently in the evening chill, what consolations would your imagination find in the prospect before you? My New England and New York experience would not forbid the hope of a private room, where I could, in the first place, wash off the dust of the road, and make some change of clothing before being admitted to a family apartment. This family room would be curtained and carpeted, and glowing softly with the light of sperm candles or a shaded lamp. When I entered it, I could expect that a couch or an arm-chair, and a fragrant cup of tea, with refined sugar, and wholesome bread of wheaten flour, leavened, would be offered me. I should think it likely that I should then have the snatch of *Tannhäuser* or *Trovatore*, which had been running faintly in my head all day, fingered clearly out to my entire satisfaction upon a piano-forte. I should then look with perfect confidence to being able to refer to Shakespeare, or Longfellow, or Dickens, if anything I had seen or thought during the day had haply led me to wish to do so. I should expect, as a matter of course, a clean, sweet bed, where I could sleep alone and undisturbed, until possibly in the morning a jug of hot water should be placed at my door, to aid the removal of a traveller's rigid beard. I should expect to draw a curtain from before a window, to lift the sash without effort, to look into a garden, and fill my lungs with fragrant air; and I should be certain when I came down of a royal breakfast. A man of these circumstances in this rich country,

he will be asking my opinion of his fruits. A man of his disposition cannot exist in the country without ladies, and ladies can not exist in the country without flowers; and might I not hope for the refinement which decks even the table with them ? and that the breakfast would be a meal as well as a feed—an institution of mental and moral sustenance as well as of palatable nourishment to the body? My horse I need hardly look after if he be a sound brute;—good stables, litter, oats, hay, and water, grooming, and discretion in their use, will never be wanting in such a man's house in the country.

In what civilized region, after such advice, would such thoughts be preposterous, unless in the Slave States ? Not but that such men and such houses, such families and home comforts may be found in the South. I have found them—a dozen of them, delightful homes. But then in a hundred cases where I received such advice, and heard houses and men so described, I did not find one of the things imagined above, nor anything ranging with them. Between the Mississippi and the upper James River, I saw not only none of those things, received none of those attentions, but I saw and met nothing of the kind. Nine times out of ten at least, after such a promise, I slept in a room with others, in a bed which stank, supplied with but one sheet, if with any ; I washed with utensils common to the whole household ; I found no garden, no flowers, no fruit, no tea, no cream, no sugar, no bread; (for corn pone, let me assert, in parenthesis, though possibly, as tastes

differ, a very good thing of its kind for ostriches, is not
bread; neither does even flour, salt, fat, and water,
stirred together and warmed, constitute bread); no cur-
tains, no lifting windows (three times out of four absolutely no windows), no couch—if one reclined in the
family room it was on the bare floor—for there were no
carpets or mats.   For all that, the house swarmed with
vermin.   There was no hay, no straw, no oats, (but
mouldy corn and leaves of maize), no discretion, no care,
no honesty at the——there was no stable, but a log-
pen; and besides this, no other out-house but a smoke-
house, a corn-house, and a range of nigger-houses.

I do not exaggerate; I cannot but err, if at all, from
a wish to avoid all possibility of exaggeration.   I say
nothing more, I am sure, than is unquestionably and
undeniably true, and exactly true, on this subject.   I
have avoided generalizations, which would cover more
ground than I can speak of with confidence from personal experience.   As to causes, we may differ; as to
facts, we cannot; for if the reader should be incredu-
lous, I will presently give him the means of satisfying
himself, that after the experience and observation of
others, who cannot be supposed prejudiced unfavora-
bly to the condition and character of the people of the
slave country, there is nothing improbable in what I
say, namely, that in nine tenths of the houses of South
Virginia, in which I was obliged, making all reasonable endeavor to find the best, to spend the night, there
were none of these things.   And most of these houses
had been recommended to me by disinterested persons

on the road as being better than ordinary—houses where
they " sot up for travellers and had things." From the
banks of the Mississippi to the banks of the James, I
did not (that I remember) see, except perhaps in one or
two towns, a thermometer, or a book of Shakespeare,
or a piano-forte or sheet of music ; or the light of a
carcel or other good centre-table or reading-lamp, or
an engraving, or a copy of any kind, of a work of art,
of the slightest merit.

Most of these houses were, I should also say, the
mansions of "planters," "slave owners," "cotton
lords," of the "Southern aristocracy." But I need not
ring the changes. If the word " planter " comes with
the same associations to the reader which it would have
formerly brought to my mind, I need say no more of
the different ideas which may be attached to the same
words in the same great country. For when has the
word "planter," in popular usage, been allowed to
stand without the company of certain other words which
hardly prepare most of us at the North for simple bacon and greens, pone and " coffee " ; which naked log-
walls, swarming with bugs ; which naked "puncheon"
floors ; which feather beds, with but one sheet, in July,
and windows without glass, in January, hardly satisfy
with men and women who have got above rag-picking or
charcoal-burning for their means of living at the North.
It is my experience that the majority of "planters,"
however broad, generous, lavish, bountiful, and luxurious may be their open-handed hospitality of
character, know of nothing better to which they can lift

open their creaking doors in welcome to the stranger guest.

Yet it is the popular opinion of the South, that the people who do the work of the North have less experience of comfort, not to say luxury, than these planters' "niggers."

Now, if the reader finds my statements of the planters' real poverty incredible, or if he imagines my experience a strangely unfortunate and exceptional one, I must beg him to review in connection the quotations given in full from Southern authorities, and chiefly from the most determined defenders of slavery and advocates of its extension, Southern born and Southern bred, in *Seaboard Slave States*.[1] Compared with these he will find that my statements have been made cautiously and with intentional moderation, that my happenings were fortunate, my experience favorable. Let him also consult Sir Charles Lyell, or the journal of any traveller who has ventured beyond hotels without letters to "first family" planters. I will here call upon just one more witness, whose evidence I cite at this point not merely because, in very few words, having reference to the very heart of the planter's prosperity, it practically endorses all I have said, but for another reason which will presently appear.

"If one unacquainted with the condition of the Southwest were told that the cotton-growing district alone had sold the crop for fifty million dollars for the last twenty years, he would

[1] Vol. I., pp. 185, 187, 192, 193, 306, 312, 323, 330; Vol. II., pp. 143, 148, 152, 156, 158, 173, 174, 179, 186, 222, 223, 371-374.

naturally conclude that this must be the richest community in the world. * * * But what would be his surprise when told that so far from living in palaces, many of these planters dwell in habitations of the most primitive construction, and these so inartificially built as to be incapable of defending the inmates from the winds and rains of heaven. That instead of any artistical improvement, this rude dwelling was surrounded by cotton fields, or probably by fields exhausted, washed into gullies, and abandoned ; that instead of canals, the navigable streams remain unimproved, to the great detriment of transportation ; that the common roads of the country were scarcely passable ; that the edifices erected for the purposes of learning and religion were frequently built of logs and covered [roofed] with boards."[1]

Do a majority of Northern working men dwell in habitations having no more elements of comfort, even taking difference of climate into consideration, than Mr. De Bow ascribes to the residences of the slaves' owners? No Northern man can for a moment hold such an opinion. What, then, becomes of the theory by which the planters justify slavery to themselves and recommend it to us ? If the ennobling luxuries which the institution of slavery secures to the " superior class," and by which it is supposed to be "qualified for the higher duties of citizenship," are, at the most, sugar, instead of molasses, in its coffee; butter, with its pone; cabbage with its bacon, and two sheets to its bed—and the traveller who goes where I travelled, month after month, with the same experience, cannot help learning to regard these as luxuries indeed,—if "freedom from sordid and petty cares," and "leisure for intellectual pursuits," means a condition approaching in comfort that of the keeper of a light-ship on an outer-bar, what

[1] J. O. B. De Bow, *Resources of the South*, vol. ii. p. 113.

is the exact value of such words as "hospitality," "generosity," and "gallantry." What is to be understood from phrases in such common use as "high toned," "well bred," "generous," "hospitable," and so on, when used in argument to prove the beneficence of slavery and to advocate its extension?

OF SOUTHERN HOSPITALITY

"Mr. Frederick Law Olmsted, after signalizing himself by two very wordy volumes, abounding in bitterness and prejudice of every sort, and misrepresentations upon the *Seaboard Slave States*, finding how profitable such literature is in a pecuniary point of view, and what a run is being made upon it throughout the entire limits of abolitiondom, vouchsafes us now another volume, entitled a *Journey through Texas, or a Saddle-trip on the Southwestern Frontier*. Here, again, the opportunity is too tempting to be resisted to revile and abuse the men and the society whose open hospitality he undoubtedly enjoyed, and whom we have no doubt, like every other of his tribe travelling at the South, he found it convenient at the time to flatter and approve. We have now grown accustomed to this, and it is not at all surprising that here and there it is producing its effect in some violent exhibition of feeling like that displayed by our worthy old friend Dr. Brewer, of Montgomery county, Maryland, who persistently refuses, on all occasions, to allow a Yankee even to cross his fields, or like that of John Randolph, who said in the House, ' Mr. Speaker, I would not allow one of my servants to buy as much as a toothorn from one of these people.' * * *

" Somewhat further on the parties rest for the night. ' For this the charge was $1.25 to each person, including breakfast and horse-feed.' At the end of every page or two our tourist repeats these growlings over the enormous exactions. It is the refrain from one cover of the book to the other. What a series of martyrdoms. Could such a journey by any possibility be made ' to pay?' Perhaps, friend traveller, you had heard of the lavish hospitality of the South, and imagined that people there moved out upon the high road for the sole purpose of sharing

the society which gentlemen, like yourself, could furnish, believing every arrival to be an act of special providence! When
you offered to pay the woman on Red River, and 'feared she
was offended by your offering her money for her hospitality,'
you paid the highest compliment to the South, for heaven
knows you would have had no such apprehension on the banks
of the Connecticut."

I cannot but be gratified that so much importance
should have been attached to the preceding volume of
this work as to induce the Superintendent of the Census to devote to its consideration a leading article in
the first economico-political review of the country, and I
can feel nothing but regret that he should be obliged to
attribute to an unworthy motive even those of my labors
the result of which he does me the honor to designate
as valuable and trustworthy. I have often had occasion
to refer to Mr. De Bow, and I believe have always done
so in a manner consistent with the respect which I feel
for the class of men among whom he has had the honorable ambition to rank himself. That a man while
occupying a position which properly belongs to the
most able and just-minded statistician in the country,
should think it proper to write under his own name in
the manner of which the above extracts are a sample,
about a work which assumes to relate calmly and me-
thodically, the result of a personal study of the condition
of the people of a certain State, is a note-worthy circumstance in illustration of the present political history of
our country. I cite them now, however, chiefly to
show what need there is for a discussion upon which I
propose to enter myself, little further than is necessary

to enable me to clearly set forth certain facts, in their important significance, the right of publishing which can hardly be denied me, in view of the insinuations made by Mr. De Bow, who in this follows what has got to be a general custom of Southern reviewers and journalists toward travellers with whose expressed judgments upon any matter observed within the Slave States they differ. There are numerous homes in the South the memory of which I cherish tenderly. There are numbers of men in the South for whom I have a warm admiration, to whom I feel grateful, whose respect I wish not to lose. There are others for whom I have a quite different feeling. Of a single individual of neither class have I spoken in these three volumes,[1] I believe, by his true name, or in such a manner that he could be recognized, or his home pointed out by any one who had not been previously familiar with it and with him, being, as a rule, careful to so far differ from the actual order of the events of my journey in narrating them, that facts of private life could not be readily localized. From this rule I do not intend now to depart further than is necessary to exhibit the whole truth of the facts to which I have referred, but since the charge of ingratitude and indelicacy is publicly máde against me, as it has frequently been of late against better men, on similar grounds, I propose to examine those grounds in the light of certain actual experiences of myself and others, and let it be judged whether there must always exist a peculiar moral obligation upon travellers to be mealy-mouthed as to the habits of the people of the South,

[1] *Seaboard Slave States, A Journey in Texas*, and *A Journey in the Back Country.*

either on account of hospitality or in reciprocation
of the delicate reserve which, from the tenor of Mr.
De Bow's remarks, it might be supposed was habitually exercised in the South with regard to the habits of
their own people. These experiences shall be both
special and general. What immediately follows is of
the former class, but, in the end, it will be found to
have a general significance.

IN OLD VIRGINIA

On a hot morning in July a Northern traveller left
the town of Lynchburg, the chief market-town of Virginia tobacco, and rode eastwardly toward Farmville.
Suddenly taken severely ill, and no house being in
sight, he turned from the road into the shade of the
wood, dismounted, reclined against a sturdy trunk, took
an anodyne, which he fortunately had with him, and
at length found relief in sleep. Late in the day he
awoke, somewhat recovered, but with a sharp headache
and much debilitated. He managed, however, to
mount, and rode slowly on to find a shelter for the
night. In half an hour the welcome sight of an old
plantation mansion greeted his eyes. There was a
large court, with shade trees and shrubbery between the
road and the house, and in the corner of this court, fac-
ing the road, a small warehouse or barn, in and around
which were a number of negroes moving casks of
tobacco. A white man, evidently their owner, was
superintending their labor, and to him the traveller applied for lodging for the night.

"We don't take in strangers."

The traveller informed the planter of his illness and inability to ride further.

"You'll have to try to ride as far as the next house, sir; we don't take in travellers here," was the reply.

"Really I don't feel able. I should not like to put you to inconvenience, sir, but I am weak and faint. My horse, too, has eaten nothing since early in the morning."

"Sorry for you, but we have no accommodations for travellers here," was the only reply, and the planter stepped to the other side of a tobacco cask.

The traveller rode on. About half an hour afterward he came in sight of another house. It was at a distance from the road, and to reach it he was obliged to let down and put up again three different sets of fence-bars. The owner was not at home, and his wife said that they were not accustomed to take in strangers. "It was not far to the next house," she added, as the traveller hesitated.

He reached, at length, the next house, which proved to be the residence of another large tobacco planter, who sat smoking in its veranda, as the traveller rode near and made his petition.

"We don't take in travellers," was again his answer.

The sick man stated his special claims to kindness, and the planter good-naturedly inquired the particulars, asked how far he had ridden, where he got his horse and his dog, whither he was bound, and so on (did not ask where he was born, or what were his poli-

tics). The traveller again stated that he was ill, unable
to ride further, and begged permission to remain for the
night under the planter's roof, and again the planter
carelessly replied that they did n't take in travellers ;
anon, asked how crops were looking further west, and
talked of guano, the war news, and the prospect for
peaches. It became dusk while the traveller lingered,
and the negroes came in with their hoes over their
shoulders from the fields across the road, but the planter
continued chatting and smoking, not even offering the
traveller a cigar, till at length the latter said, "If you
really cannot keep me to-night I must go on, sir ; I cannot keep my horse much longer, I fear."

"It is not far to the next house."

"But I have already called at three houses to-night,
sir."

"Well, you see, since the railroad was done, people
here don't reckon to take in travellers as they once did.
So few come along they don't find their account in being ready for them."

The traveller asked for a drink of water, which a
negro brought in a calabash, bade good night to the
planter, and rode on through the woods. Night presently set in ; the road crossed a swamp and was difficult
to follow, and for more than an hour he rode on—seeing no house—without stopping. Then crossing water,
he deliberated whether he should not bivouac for the
night where he was. He had with him a few biscuits
and some dried figs. He had not eaten hitherto, hoping constantly to come to a habitation where it might

happen he could get a cup of tea, of which he felt more particularly in need. He stopped, took some nourishment, the first he had tasted in fifteen hours, and taking also a little brandy, gained strength and courage to continue his journey. A bright light soon cheered him, and after a time he made his way to a large white house, in the rear of which was an old negro woman stirring the contents of a cauldron which stood over the fire, by which he had been guided. The old woman had the appearance of a house servant, and he requested her to ask her master if he would favor him with lodging for the night.

"Her master did not take in travellers," she said, "besides, he was gone to bed"; and she stirred on, hardly looking at the traveller till he put his hand in his pocket, and, holding forth silver, said:

"Now, aunty, mind what I tell you. Do you go in to your master and say to him, 'There is a gentleman outside who says he is sick, and that his horse is tired and has had nothing to eat to-day; that he is a stranger and has been benighted, don't know the roads, is not well enough to ride further, and wants to know if you won't be so kind as to let him stay here to-night.'"

"Yes, massa, I'll tell him; 't won't do no good, though, and he'll be almighty cross."

She went in, returned after a few minutes, seized her paddle, and began stirring before she uttered the words, "Says yer ken go on to de store, he reckon."

It was after ten o'clock when the traveller reached

the next house.   It stood close upon the road, and the voice of a woman answered a knock upon the door, and in reply to the demand, said it was not far to the store and she reckoned they accommodated travellers there.

Finally, at the store, the traveller succeeded in getting admittance, was comfortably lodged, and well entertained by an amiable family. Their kindness was of such a character that he felt in the position of an invited guest, unable to demand and unwilling to suggest any unvolunteered service. There was no indication that the house was an inn, yet the traveller's experience left him little room to hesitate to offer money, nor was there the slightest hesitation on the part of the store-keeper in naming the amount due for the entertainment he had, or in taking it.

If the reader will accept the traveller's judgment of himself, he will assume that there was nothing in his countenance, his dress, his language, or his bearing, by which he could readily be distinguished from a gentleman of Southern birth and education, and that he was not imagined to be anything else, certainly not on his first inquiry, at any one of the plantations where he was thus refused shelter.

So far as this inhospitality (for this is, I think, what even the Southern reader will be inclined to call it) needed explanation, it was supposed to be sufficiently given in the fact that the region had, by the recent construction of a railroad through it, approximated the condition of a well-settled and organized community, in which the movements of travellers are so systema-

tized, that the business of providing for their wants, as a matter of pecuniary profit, can no longer be made a mere supplement of another business, but becomes a distinct occupation.

This, then, but a small part of the whole land being thus affected by railroads, was an exception in the South. True; but what is the rule to which this is the exception?

Mr. De Bow says, that the traveller would have had no apprehension that the offer of money for chance entertainment for the night furnished him at a house on the banks of the Connecticut, would give offense; yet in the Connecticut valley, among people having no servants, and not a tithe of the nominal wealth of the Red River planter, or of one of these Virginia planters, such has been a frequent experience of the same traveller. Nor has he ever, when calling benighted at a house, anywhere in the State of Connecticut, far from a public house, escaped being invited with cordial frankness to enjoy such accommodation as it afforded; and this, he is fully convinced, without any thought in the majority of cases of pecuniary remuneration. In several instances a remuneration in money has been refused in a manner which conveyed a reproof of the offer of it as indelicate; and it thus happens that it was a common experience of that, of the possibility of which Mr. De Bow is unable to conceive, that led in no small degree to the hesitation upon which this very comment was made.

This simple faith in the meanness of the people of

the North, and especially of New England, is no eccentricity of Mr. De Bow's. It is in accordance with the general tone of literature and of conversation at the South, that penuriousness, disingenuousness, knavish cunning, cant, and hypocrisy, are assumed to be the prevailing traits by which they are distinguished from the people of the South—not the poor people of New England from the planters of the South, but the people generally from the people generally. Not the tone of the political literature and of the lower class of the South, but of its wealthy class, very generally, really of its "better class." Mr. De Bow is himself the associate of gentlemen as well informed and as free from narrow prejudices as any in the South. No New England man, who has travelled at the South, would be surprised, indeed, if, at a table at which he were a guest, such an assumption as that of Mr. De Bow should be apparent in all the conversation ; that the gist of it should be supposed to be so well understood and generally conceded, that he could not be annoyed by its plainest statement.

I need hardly say that this reference to Mr. De Bow is continued, not for the purpose of vindicating the North any more than myself from a mistaken criticism. I wish only to demonstrate how necessary it must soon be to find other means for saving the Union than these common-place flatteries of Southern conceit and apologies for Southern folly, to which we have not only become so accustomed ourselves, as to hardly believe our eyes when we are obliged to meet the facts (as was my

own case), but by which we have so successfully imposed upon our friends, that a man like Mr. De Bow
actually supposes that the common planters of the teem-
ing and sunny South, are, as a rule, a more open-
handed, liberal, and hospitable class than the hard-
working farmers of the bleak and sterile hills of New
England; so much so that he feels warranted not merely
in stating facts within his personal knowledge, illus-
trating the character of the latter and arguing the
causes, but in incidentally referring to their penuriousness as a matter of proverbial contempt. Against this
mistake, which, I doubt not, is accomplishing constant
mischief to our nation, I merely oppose the facts of
actual experience. I wish to do so with true respect
for the good sense of the South.

IN GENERAL

Presenting myself and known only in the character
of a chance traveller, most likely to be in search of
health, entertainment, and information, usually taken
for and treated as a Southerner, until I stated that I
was not one, I journeyed nearly six months at one time
(my second journey) through the South. During all
this journey, I came not oftener than once a week, on
an average, to public houses, and was thus generally
forced to seek lodging and sustenance at private houses.
Often it was refused me; not unfrequently rudely refused. But once did I meet with what Northern readers
could suppose Mr. De Bow to mean by the term (used
in the same article) " free road-side hospitality." Not

once with the slightest appearance of what Noah Webster defines hospitality, the "practice of receiving or
entertaining strangers without reward."

Only twice, in a journey of four thousand miles, made
independently of public conveyances, did I receive a
night's lodging or a repast from a native Southerner,
without having the exact price in money which I was
expected to pay for it stated to me by those at whose
hands I received it.

If what I have just narrated had been reported to me
before I travelled in the manner I did in my second
journey at the South, I should have had serious doubts
of either the honesty or the sanity of the reporter. I
know, therefore, to what I subject myself in now giving my own name to it. I could not but hesitate to do
this, as one would be cautious in acknowledging that
he believed himself to have seen the sea-serpent, or had
discovered a new motive power. By drawing out the
confidence of other travellers, who had chanced to move
through the South in a manner at all similar, however,
I have had the satisfaction of finding that I am not altogether solitary in my experience. Even this day I
met one fresh from the Southwest, to whom, after due
approach, I gave the article which is the text of these
observations, asking to be told how he had found it in
New England and in Mississippi. He replied:

"During four winters, I have travelled for a business purpose two months each winter in Mississippi. I have generally spent the night at houses with whose inmates I had some
previous acquaintance. Where I had business transactions,

especially where debts were due me, which could not be paid, I sometimes neglected to offer payment for my night's lodging, but in no other case, and never in a single instance, so far as I can now recollect, where I had offered payment, has there been any hesitation in taking it. A planter might refrain from asking payment of a traveller, but it is universally expected. In New England, as far as my limited experience goes, it is not so. I have known New England farmers' wives take a small gratuity after lodging travellers, but always with apparent hesitation. I have known New England farmers refuse to do so. I have had some experience in Iowa; money is there usually (not always) taken for lodging travellers. The principal difference between the custom at private houses there and in Alabama and Mississippi being that in Iowa the farmer seems to carefully reckon the exact value of the produce you have consumed, and to charge for it at what has often seemed to me an absurdly low rate ; while in Mississippi, I have usually paid from four to six times as much as in Iowa, for similar accommodations. I consider the usual charges of planters to travellers extortionate, and the custom the reverse of hospitable. I knew of a Kentucky gentleman travelling from Eutaw to Greensboro [twenty miles] in his own conveyance. He was taken sick at the crossing of the Warrior River. It was nine o'clock at night. He averred to me that he called at every plantation on the road, and stated that he was a Kentuckian, and sick, but was refused lodging at each of them."

This the richest county of Alabama, and the road is lined with valuable plantations.

The following is an extract from a letter dated Columbus, Mississippi, November 24, 1856, published in the London *Daily News*. It is written by an Englishman travelling for commercial purposes, and tells what he has learned by experience of the custom of the country.

"It is customary in travelling through this country, where towns are few and taverns scarce and vile, to stop at the plant-

ers' houses along the road, and pay for your bed and board in
the morning just as if you had staid at an inn. The custom is
rather repugnant to our Old World notions of hospitality, but
it appears to me an excellent one for both the host and his
guest. The one feels less bored by demands upon his kindness,
as soon as it ceases to be merely a kindness to comply with
them, and the other has no fear about intruding or being
troublesome when he knows he will have to pay for his entertainment. It is rarely, however, that the *entrée* can be obtained
into the houses of wealthy planters in this way. They will not
be bothered by your visits and if you apply to them, have no
hesitation in politely passing you on to such of their neighbors
as have less money or more generosity."

The same writer afterwards relates the following
experience:

"About nineteen miles from Canton, I sought lodging at
nightfall at a snug house on the roadside, inhabited by an old
gentleman and his two daughters, who possessed no slaves and
grew no cotton, and whose two sons had been killed in the
Mexican war, and who, with the loudest professions of hospitality, cautiously refrained from giving himself any personal
trouble in support of them. He informed me that there was
corn in the husk in an almost inaccessible loft, there was fodder
in an un-get-at-able sort of a cage in the yard, water in a certain
pond about half a mile off, and a curry comb in a certain hole in
the wall. Having furnished me with this intelligence, he left
me to draw my own conclusions as to what my conduct ought
to be under the circumstances."

A naturalist, the author of a well known standard
work, who has made several tours of observation in
the Slave States, lately confided to me that he believed
that the popular report of Southern hospitality must be
a popular romance, for never, during all his travels in
the South, had he chanced to be entertained for a single night, except by gentlemen to whom he was form-
ally presented by letter, or who had previously been

under obligations to him, without paying for it in money, and to an amount quite equal to the value received. By the wealthier, a night's entertainment had been frequently refused him, under circumstances which, as must have been evident to them, rendered his further progress seriously inconvenient. Once, while in company with a foreign naturalist—a titled man—he had been dining at the inn of a small county-town, when a certain locally distinguished judge had seen fit to be eloquent at the dinner-table upon the advantages of slavery in maintaining a class of "high-toned gentlemen," referring especially to the proverbial hospitality of Southern plantations, which he described as quite a bewilderment to strangers, and nothing like which was to be found in any country unblessed with slavery, or institutions equivalent to it. It so happened that the following night the travellers, on approaching a plantation mansion in quest of lodging, were surprised to find that they had fallen upon the residence of this same judge, who recognized them, and welcomed them and bade them be at home. Embarrassed by a recollection of his discourse of hospitality, it was with some difficulty that one of them, when they were taking leave next morning, brought himself to inquire what he might pay for the entertainment they had received. He was at once relieved by the judge's prompt response, "Dollar and a quarter apiece, I reckon."

It is very true that the general custom of the South which leads a traveller to ask for a lodging at any pri-

vate house he may chance to reach near nightfall, and
to receive a favorable answer not merely as a favor but
as a matter of business, is a convenient one, is one
indeed almost necessary in a country so destitute of
villages, and where, off certain thoroughfares of our
merchants, there are so few travellers. It is a perfectly
respectable and entirely sensible custom, but it is not,
as it is commonly represented to be, a custom of hospitality, and it is not at all calculated to induce customs
of hospitality with the mass of citizens. It is calculated to make inhospitality of habit and inhospitality
of character the general rule ; hospitality of habit and
of character the exception. Yet the common misap-
plication of the word to this custom is, so far as I can
ascertain, the only foundation of the arrogant assumption of superiority of character in this respect of the
Southerners over ourselves—the only ground of the
claim that slavery breeds a race of more generous and
hospitable citizens than freedom.

OF SOUTHERN BREEDING

The difficulty of giving any thing like an intelligent
and exact estimate of the breeding of any people or of
any class of people is almost insurmountable, owing to
the vagueness of the terms which must be used, or
rather to the quite different ideas which different readers will attach to these terms. The very word which
I have employed to designate my present subject has
itself such a varied signification that it needs to be
defined at the outset. I mean to employ it in that

sense wherein, according to Webster, it covers the
ground of "nurture, instruction, and the formation of
manners." It is something more than "manners and
customs," then, and includes or may include qualities
which, if not congenital, are equally an essential part
of character with those qualities which are literally
inbred of a man. Such qualities are mainly the result
of a class of circumstances, of the influence of which
upon his character and manners a man, or a child
growing to a man, is usually unconscious, and of
which he cannot be independent if he would.

The general difficulty is increased in dealing with the
people of the Slave States, because among themselves
all terms defining social rank and social characteristics
are applied in a manner which can be understood only
after considerable experience ; and also because the
general terms of classification, always incomplete in
their significance, fail entirely with a large class of
Southerners, whose manners have some characteristics
which would elsewhere be thought "high bred," if
they had not others which are elsewhere universally
esteemed low and ruffianly.

I do not feel myself competent, therefore, to thoroughly analyze Southern breeding ; but I propose,
while giving my impressions for what they may be
considered worth, and claiming but little value for
them, to demonstrate clearly the error of certain views
on this subject, which have been popularly held at the
South, and are still advanced with great confidence by
many writers and orators.

There are undoubted advantages resulting from the
effects of slavery upon the manners of some persons.
The same results to manners, the same sort of breeding, I have thought that I perceived to have arisen in
the Free States, where a family has been educated
with every advantage which wealth would be likely to
secure, when judiciously used, in a frontier community.
There is boldness, directness, largeness, confidence,
with the effect of the habitual sense of superiority to
most of the community ; not superiority of wealth, and
power from wealth merely, but of a mind well-stocked
and refined by such advantages of education as only
very unusual wealth can procure in a scattered and
frontier community.   When to this is added the effect
of visits to the society of the wealthy of denser communities ; when refined and polished manners are
grafted on a natural, easy abandon ; when there is high
culture without effeminacy either of body or mind, as
not unfrequently happens, we find a peculiarly respectable and agreeable sort of men and women.   They are
the result of frontier training under the most favorable
circumstances.   In the class furthest removed from
this on the frontier —people who have grown up without civilized social restraints or encouragements, and
always under what in a well-conditioned community
would be esteemed great privations—happens, on the
other hand, the most disagreeable specimen of mankind that the world breeds ; men of a sort almost peculiar to America and Australia ; border ruffians, of whom
the "rowdies" of our Eastern towns are tame reflec-

tions. Cooper has well described the first class in many instances. I know of no picture of the latter which represents them as detestable as I have found them.

The whole South is maintained in a frontier condition by the system which is apologized for on the ground that it favors good breeding. This system, at the same time, tends to concentrate wealth in a few hands. If there is wisdom and great care in the education of a family thus favored, the result which we see at the North, under the circumstances I have described, is frequently reproduced. This is the whole story of the advantages of slavery on manners. There are many more such fruits of frontier life at the South than the North, because there is more frontier life. There is also vastly more of the other sort, and there is everything between, which degrees of wealth and degrees of good fortune in education would be expected to occasion. The bad breed of the frontier, at the South, however, is probably far worse than that of the North, because any effort toward something better which it may be inclined to make, is so effectually snubbed in most cases by the tendencies described in a former chapter and because the frontier condition of the South is everywhere permanent. The child born to-day on the Northern frontier, in most cases, before it is ten years old, will be living in a well organized and tolerably well provided community ; schools, churches, libraries, lecture and concert halls, daily mails and printing presses, shops and machines in variety, hav-

ing arrived within at least a day's journey of it, being always within an influencing distance of it. There are improvements, and communities loosely and gradually cohering in various parts of the South, but so slowly, so feebly, so irregularly, that men's minds and habits are knit firm quite independently of this class of social influences.

There is one other grand ruling characteristic of the Southerner, which I here state as a fact, without pretending to state it clearly, and without undertaking to account for it, merely observing that it is far more decided than the difference of climate merely would warrant. It is intensity of impulse—willfulness. Every wish of the Southerner is, for the moment at least, more imperative than of the Northerner, every belief more undoubted, every hate more vengeful, every love more fiery. Hence, for instance, the scandalous fiend-like street fights of the South. If a young man feels offended with another, he does not incline to a ring and a fair stand-up set-to, like a young Englishman ; he will not attempt to overcome his opponent by logic ; he will not be content to vituperate, or to cast ridicule upon him ; he is impelled straightway to kill him with the readiest deadly weapon at hand, and with as little ceremony and pretence of fair combat as the loose organization of the people against violence will allow. He seems crazy for blood. Intensity of personal pride —pride in anything a man has, or which connects itself with him, is more commonly evident; hence intense partizanship ; hence rashness and overconfidence ;

hence visionary ambition; hence assurance and violence
in debate; hence assurance in society : no matter how
ignorant, how out of place, self-assurance seldom fails
—partisan assurance never. As self-appreciation is
equally with deference a part of what we call good
breeding, and as the expression of deference is much
more easily reduced to a matter of manners and forms,
in the common-place intercourse of society, than
self-appreciation, this characteristic quality of the
Southerner needs to be borne in mind in considering
the port and manners he commonly has, and judging
from them of the effects of slavery. What a man
shows that he thinks of himself is certainly of considerable consequence in estimating his value to others.
But it is not everything, or most essential. What he
wishes to be, labors to be, is, perhaps, of more consequence, and this is not to be as quickly and as
certainly understood from his own presentation of
himself.

This much I have written in explanation of what is
usually assumed by Southerners to be the common
opinion of the superior breeding of the South. I will
now consider what is the general fact.

In the North, at the Revolution, we scarcely had a
distinct class corresponding to the lowest white class
of Virginia, as described by Jefferson, our laborers being less ignorant and coarse in their habits, and associating much more familiarly with their betters. We
have now a class more nearly corresponding to it, furnished by the European peasant immigration. It is,

however, a transient class, somewhat seldom including
two generations, and, on an average, I trust, not one.
It is, therefore, practically not an additional class, but,
overlooking the aged and diseased, a supplement to our
lowest normal class.   Out of twenty Irish proletaires,
of whose history for five years after their arrival and removal to the country I have been intimately cognizant,
only two, both of whom were over fifty years of age,
have lived out that period without beginning to acquire
wealth and becoming superior in their ambition and
habits to the lowest order, which I believe to include a
majority of the whites in the plantation districts of the
South.[1] Our lowest class, therefore, has a higher standard than the lowest class of the Slave States.   This, I
understand, is made very evident where the two come
together at the West, as in Southern Illinois.   The
very poorest and lowest New England women who
go there, are frequently offended by the inconsiderate
rudeness and coarseness of the women immigrating from
the South, and shocked by their "shiftless," comfort-
less, vagrant habits, so much so that families have
often removed, after having been once established, to
escape being bored and annoyed by their Southern-
born neighbors.

Referring to the lowest class, North and South, as

[1] I fear that it must be confessed that this general rule has
now a multitude of exceptions in our large towns, where, in
New York, especially, we seem taking some pains to form a
permanent lower class.   With the present great and apparently
permanent falling off in the European emigration, it can hardly
last, however.

the fourth, I class as third, the lowest rank in society, North or South, in which regard is had by its members to the quality of their associates from other than moral motives, or the prejudices of locality, race, sectarianism, and politics. In other words, that in which there is a distinct social selectiveness and pride. I think that everywhere in the Free States men of this class would almost universally feel their position damaged—be a little ashamed—if obliged to confess that they did not take a newspaper, or were unable to read it with a clear understanding of the intelligence it was intended to communicate. Allusions to the main facts of American history, to any clause of the Bible, to the provisions of the Constitution, and the more important laws, State and national, would be understood in most cases by those whom I refer to as the third class in Northern society. In few families of this class would you fail to find some volumes of the English poets, or some works of great novelists or renowned travellers. Nothing like this would you find in the third class at the South.

The ratio of the number of the citizens who cannot read at all to the whole, appears, by the census returns, to be only three times larger at the South than at the North. I believe it to be much greater at the South than these returns indicate.[1] The comparative cultiva-

---

[1] The ratio of white illiterate to white population, per cent., as returned, is,

$\begin{cases} \text{Free States, } 3.36 \\ \text{Slave } \text{``} \quad 8.27 \end{cases}$; of the native population, over 20 years old, it is,

$\begin{cases} \text{Free States, } 4.12 \\ \text{Slave } \text{``} \quad 17.23 \end{cases}$; (*Census Compendium*, pp. 152, 153.) The

tion of the third class "North" and of the third class "South," however, cannot be at all judged from these statistics, supposing them correct. Those who can read and who do not read, or whose reading is confined within extremely narrow limits, are a much larger number at the South than at the North, owing to the much poorer supply of books and newspapers which commerce can afford to put within the reach of the former. The census returns two million newspapers, for instance, printed annually in Virginia, one hundred and fifteen million in New York. There is a post office to every fourteen square miles in New York, one to forty-seven square miles in Virginia; over five hundred publishers and booksellers in New York, but forty in Virginia. Thirty thousand volumes in public libraries in Virginia, eight hundred thousand in New York. The area occupied by the population of Virginia being much the largest, it may be inferred that with the disposition and the ability to read anything in particular, the Virginian of the third class will have to travel more than thirty times as far as the New Yorker to procure it. The same proposition will hold good in regard to most other means of cultivation, and the third class of the South generally has seemed to me to be as much more narrow-minded, rude, coarse, "dangerous," and miserable, than the third class of the Free States, as the most

---

ability to merely read and write may itself be of little value, but the fact of a child's having had the pains-taking necessary to so far instruct him is in some degree a means of measuring his other inherited wealth, and thus his breeding.

sanguine friend of popular education could anticipate from these facts.

The great difference in character between the third class of the South and that of the North, as indicated by their respective manners, is found in the much less curiosity and ready intelligent interest in matters which have not an immediate personal bearing in that of the South. Apathetic carelessness rather than simple indifference, or reckless incivility as to your comfort, is what makes the low Southerner a disagreeable companion. It is his impertinent shrewdness which makes you wish to keep the Yankee at a distance. The first seems without object, spiritless ; the latter keen to better himself, if with nothing else, with information which he can draw from you, and by gaining your good opinion.

The next or second class would include, both North and South, those with whose habits and character I am most familiar, and of whom I can speak with the best right to confidence. It would include in New England and New York the better educated farmers—these owning, I should say, half the agricultural land—the permanently established manufacturers and merchants of moderate capital ; most of the shop-keepers and better-educated master mechanics and artisan foremen ; most of the preachers, physicians, and lawyers (some ranking higher). It would correspond most nearly to what in England would be called the lower-middle class, but any higher grade being very ill-defined, existing distinctly but in few localities, and rarely recognized as

existing at all, it is in a great measure free from the
peculiar vulgarity of its English parallel.

The number of those at the South who correspond
in education and refinement of manners and habits to
the average of this class of the North, it will be evident
from a similar mode of reasoning to that before employed, must be very much smaller relatively, either to
the territory or the whole white population of their
respective regions.

In the comparison commonly made by Southern
writers between the condition of the people of a sparsely
settled country and another, it is usually assumed that
the advantages of the latter are confined exclusively to
towns, and to large and crowded towns. By contrasting
the evils which concentrate in such towns with the favorable circumstances of life, where at least wood, water,
and air are abundant, and corn is usually comparatively cheap, an argument of some force to ignorant
people is easily presented. The advantages possessed
by a people living in communities, or in moderately
well occupied rural districts, who are even more free
from the evils of great towns than their own people,
are entirely overlooked by most Southern writers.
Such is the condition, however, of more white people
in the Free States than the whole white population of
the Slave States. A majority of our farmers' daughters
can walk from their dwellings to schools of a quality
such as at the South can be maintained not twice in
five hundred square miles. These schools are practically a part of their homes. Probably, in more than

half the families of the South, the children of which are
instructed to the least degree which would be considered "respectable," among this second class of the
North, private governesses are obliged to be employed,
or the children must be for many years at boarding-
schools. We all know that the young women who go
to the South, to meet the demand thus occasioned for
home education, are not generally, though they may
be in cases, our own most esteemed and successful in-
structresses; and we also know from their report that
their skill and labor has necessarily to be long chiefly
employed in laying those simple foundation habits of
instructability, which our Northern children acquire
imperceptibly from association with those of the neighborhood slightly in advance of them. Churches and
the various sub-organizations centering in them, in
which class distinctions are much lost sight of, to the
great advantage of the manners of the lower classes,
and little chance of injury to the higher; libraries,
literary societies, lecture arrangements, dramatic and
musical, art and scientific entertainments, and also
highly educated professional men, with whom, for various purposes, many persons are brought often in contact, are correspondingly more frequent at the North,
correspondingly more accessible; in other words, the
advantages to be derived from them are cheaper, and
so more influential on the manners of the people at
large.

The common opinion has been that the Southerners
or planters of the class now under consideration, are

more social, more generous, more heartily kind and
genial than Northerners. According to my experience, the reverse of all this is true, as a general rule.
Families live so isolated at the South, that any social
contact, out of the family, is of course much more
eventful and stimulating than it is ordinarily at the
North, and this accounts for the common opinion. I
could not but think, however, that most persons at the
South looked to the voluntary good offices and conversation of others, both within and without their
families, for their enjoyment of the world, much less
than most at the North. It may be that when in towns
they attach a greater value to, and are more careful to
make use of the opportunities for social gatherings afforded by towns, than are Northerners. In towns they
attach more consequence to forms, are more scrupulous
in matters of etiquette, more lavish in expenditure for
dress, and for certain other things which are the signs
of luxury rather than luxury itself, such as plate and
fancy brands of wines. They make less show of fine
art, and less pretense of artistic judgment.

As to manner or deportment simply, with the same
impulse and intention, that of the Southerner will be
best, more true, more quiet, more modestly self-assured,
more dignified. I have said that the second class at
the North is without the pervading vulgarity of the class
to which it most nearly corresponds in England, the
reason being that those which constitute it seldom wish
or attempt to appear to belong to a superior class, not
clearly recognizing a superior class. Individuals, how-

ever, very generally have a strong desire to be thought
better informed, more ingenious, more witty, as well
as more successful in their enterprises than they are,
and this stamps them with a peculiar quality of manners vulgarly called "smartness," the absence of
which makes Southern men and women generally much
more agreeable companions than Northerners of the
same degree of education and accomplishments in other
respects.   Not but that snobs abound ; of these it will
be more convenient to speak under the next division,
however.

We have next to consider the somewhat famous First
Families.

The traditional "family," stately but condescending,
haughty but jovial, which has long kept open house for
all comers on the old plantations of Virginia or South
Carolina, is not wholly a myth.

There really was something which, with some sort
of propriety, could be termed a gentry in Carolina and
Virginia in their colony days ; yet of the names which
are now thought to have belonged to it, as descended of
brave, loyal, and adventurous cavaliers, some I once
saw in London upon an old freight-list of a ship out-
ward bound for Virginia, with the addition of tinker and
tailor, poacher and pickpocket, all to be sold for life, or a
term of years, to the highest bidder when they should
arrive.

What was properly to be termed the gentry in Virginia and South Carolina previous to the Revolution,
was much smaller in number than is, I believe, com-

monly supposed. A large proportion of the families
who composed it and who remained after the Revolution in the country (for many were Tories), have since
passed in all their branches through a poverty-stricken
period, very dissipating in its influence upon hereditary
breeding, novelists and dramatic old servants to the
contrary notwithstanding. Many of those who have
retained wealth and family pride in succession to the
present time, have undeniably, from various causes, de-
generated wofully in breeding. Coarse tastes and brutal dispositions cannot be disguised under a cavalier
address, and the most assured readiness in the established forms of polite society. Of the real "old families" which remain at all "high bred" in their qualities, habits, and manners, I think it will be difficult for
most readers who have not studied the matter at all to
form a sufficiently small estimate. Some may be supposed, however. Associating with these are many new
or recuperated families, in which there is also the best
breeding, and in certain few parts or districts of the
South, to be defined and numbered without difficulty,
there is unquestionably a wealthy and remarkably generous, hospitable, refined, and accomplished first-class,
clinging with some pertinacity, although with too evident an effort, to the traditional manners and customs
of an established gentry. I speak of them as a class
with some question of the propriety of the term,
for I do not much doubt that, as I was told at the
South, old ladies may easily be found who will give
you a complete census of the whole really "first

class people," between the courses of a well-served dinner.

There was a gentry in the North as well as in Virginia and Carolina in the colony period, though a less important and more numerous one. As the North has been much more prosperous, as the value of its property has much more rapidly increased than that of the South, the advantages of wealth have, I believe, been more generally retained in families, and probably the number of those who could trace their breeding in an uninterrupted parental influence from the colonial gentry, is now larger at the North than the South.

Including new families, in whose habits and manners and conversation the best bred people of Europe would find nothing more offensive and inharmonious with themselves than might be ascribed to local fashion or a desire to avoid the responsibility of social leadership, there is unquestionably at this time a very much larger number of thoroughly well bred and even high bred people in the Free than in the Slave States. It is equally certain that the proportion of such people to the whole population of whites is larger at the North than the South.

The great majority of wealthy planters who at the present day assume for themselves a special social respectability and superiority to the class I have defined as the second, are, as a general rule, not only distinguished for all those qualities which our satirists and dramatists are accustomed to assume to be the especial property of the newly rich of the Fifth Avenue, but, as

far as I have had opportunity to observe both classes, are
far more generally and ridiculously so than the would-
be fashionable people of New York, or of any other
part of the United States.   It is a part of the *rôle* they
undertake to act, to be hospitable and generous, as it
was lately that of our fops to be sleepy and critical.
They are not hospitable and generous, however ; they
know not the meaning of these terms.   They are absurdly ostentatious in entertainment, and extravagant
in the purchase of notoriety ; possibly they have more
tact in this than our Potiphars, but such has not been
my personal observation.

It is only at a few centers of commerce in the South
that there is a permanent class of merchants and functionaries such as chiefly lead in Northern society, and
at these the characteristics of society are foreign.
With the lawyers, merchants, and functionaries of the
Interior of the South, I have had little to do.   I judge
them to be superior very much to the planting class, on
an average, yet in several instances where I have been
introduced to them, I have found them to be of such
habits and manners as would have prevented them from
occupying satisfactorily, similar stations at the North.
Speaking of merchants, I am reminded of an amusing
experience in my journey, which I relate not so much
with the intention of instructing the reader as to the
mercantile customs of the South, as for his entertainment.   It illustrates, however, the wonderful liberality
and hospitality to strangers which is supposed to be only
born of slavery.

Changing my plans of travel in Mississippi, I pursued a route to Virginia for which I had not previously provided myself with letters. The day after I reached Tuscaloosa I asked advice of the landlord of my inn as to how I could best obtain money by drafts on New York. He seemed surprised at the inquiry; there was but one man who was known to do anything like an exchange business in the town. On this man, who had some title, judge or governor, I think, I accordingly called. He told me that he was in the habit of selling drafts on New York; they had a certain value when any one wished to pay a bill there. I stated my circumstances, and with much difficulty got him to examine various letters which I carried with me; some of them were from distinguished men, both of the North and South, with whom he professed to have an acquaintance. He did not for a moment doubt that I was the man I assumed to be, or that I was " good " for a much larger amount than I desired him to favor me with. He politely informed me that he did not make a business of furnishing money to travellers; and when I asked if he could not recommend me to some one in the town who would so far accommodate me, he said that he did not think I would find any one to do so. I reminded him that this would leave me in a very unpleasant predicament. He was sorry for it, he replied, but he did not see that he could help it, and as he had other business he would wish me good morning. I called with no better success upon two merchants, and then making a close calculation, I concluded that with

good luck I could pay my way, by travelling in the most carefully frugal manner on the course I intended pursuing, to Chattanooga in Tennessee, and that by the time I reached that point I might expect to be supplied with funds in answer to a letter.

I succeeded in reaching Chattanooga, but with quite an empty purse. My letters informed me that I was accredited to the postmaster. This gentleman received me cordially, and at once offered to introduce me to the bank. At the bank, after a little general conversation with a polite cashier, I asked him to cash a draft on New York for two hundred dollars. He withdrew, and presently desired to see the postmaster in a private apartment. Soon after this, I was called in and presented to the president, who, after some polite inquiries about my health, wished to know what friend I had in town who could identify me. None, but here was the postmaster with a letter— Ah! but what assurance had they—(that this letter had not been sent the postmaster by an accomplice, he meant); how, in fact, it was mildly asked, was it to be known that I was not a swindler? I presented a circular letter of credit of Duncan, Sherman & Co. on their Mexican correspondents, and a general letter of credence by the Governor of New York. But who knew their signatures to be genuine, who could identify me as the Frederick Law Olmsted spoken of in them? I offered to show various letters of introduction and twenty letters received by me at post offices on the route which I alleged that I had followed from Mexico; I proposed to show the marks on my

linen, my engraved cards, my Mexican passport. But how were they to be made secure that I came honestly by these things? It was my intention to remain a day or two, would I be so good as to leave my letters and papers, and allow them time for consideration?

When I called again at the banking establishment, which was a very commodious and handsome one, the cashier received me with consideration. They had had a meeting of their directors, he said, at which my request had been the subject of debate, and it had been determined, in as much as it seemed that I would not otherwise be able to pursue my journey, to cash a draft on New York for me, but the directors thinking that two hundred dollars was a larger amount than I should find absolutely necessary, he was only authorized to furnish me with one hundred, which he accordingly did in new notes of the bank.

I was subsequently kept in funds by Southern banknotes, bought in New York and sent by mail to a designated point on my route.

Of course, there was nothing wrong in all this—or if there was, it was with myself and my friends—but if a Southerner had had anything like such an experience in New England, would he have said nothing about wooden nutmegs, and so forth? Comparisons of this kind are anything but agreeable to draw. They will be necessary, however, and it will be necessary that the removal of much popular delusion be seriously and systematically undertaken, if the future discussion of the slavery question is to have the character which, of late,

Southern writers have attempted to give it. I find no
more foundation for the assumption of a greater habitual liberality or a more thorough-going honesty, than
of a more general hospitality having been produced by
slavery, even upon the planters, than exists among ourselves. To say nothing more of my personal experience,
I will drop this disagreeable subject after giving two
short paragraphs from Southern newspapers, and a
third, merely by way of explanation, from a foreign
periodical.

RELIGIOUS CONTRIBUTIONS

"In looking over the annual statement of the Board of Foreign Missions, there is a fact that strikes us painfully. By
summing up the entire contributions of the Synod of Virginia,
we find them to be $3,475.65. Those of the Synod of North
Carolina amount to $5,000.90. By referring to the report of
contributions from New York, we find that the First Church
(Dr. Philips') has given $6,386.60, and the Fifth Avenue and
Nineteenth Street (Dr. Alexander's), $7,648.74—each of them
more than all the churches in both of these Synods! Brethren,
why is this? Is one church in New York richer than both
these large and prosperous Synods? Why, then, this fact?"—
Richmond Central Herald.

THE HONEST PLANTER AT HOME

"The editor of *The Savannah Republican* is in receipt of a letter from one of the cotton manufacturing companies in Georgia,
mentioning the purchase of a crop of cotton at Macon, which,
from actual weight, contained fifty-five per cent. of sand, leaving but forty-five per cent. of cotton."

THE HONEST PLANTER ABROAD

Ten Million Dollars Per Annum

"When the spinner comes to open and inspect his purchases

at the mill, he frequently finds concealed therein substances
which are certainly not cotton.   Formerly flint stones were the
principal articles selected as substitutes ; and the manufacturer
used often to discover that instead of the 'fair bowed ' which
he had bought and paid for, he was favored with a considerable
weight of geological specimens.   But it seems at length to have
struck certain individuals on the other side of the Atlantic, that
this was at best but a coarse and vulgar fraud, unworthy of an
enlightened age and people, and that it was possible to carry out
the principle of sophistication on a far more extended scale,
and in a much more refined manner.

"Accordingly the system of 'sanding' sprung up, and instead of bales consisting of American cotton they are frequently
found to consist of America itself, to the extent of ten, twenty,
or in many instances of more than thirty per cent.

"The extent to which this practice has reached may be imagined when it is known that, taking the adulteration at ten per
cent. on the import of the last crop, which is stated to be a very
low estimate, a quantity of sand equal in weight to more than two
hundred thousand bales, or forty thousand tons, is found to
have been bought and paid for as cotton by Great Britain, *at an
expense of upwards of £2,000,000* sterling ; and that there are
now lying at Liverpool at least one hundred thousand
bales of this sanded cotton which spinners will not buy at any
price.

" But it may be asked, 'Cannot they purchase it at an allow-
ance in price proportionate to the amount of adulteration?'
To this it must be answered that cotton is now bought by sample and not by inspection of the bulk of the article, which
indeed would be almost impracticable from the nature of the
packages and other causes.   When the cotton is warehoused, on
its arrival from abroad, a sample is taken from each of the
bales, but these are pressed so hard that it is impossible to pene-
trate more than a few inches into them.   If, therefore, as is
generally the case, the surface layer be clean cotton, it is evident that the sample can be of no value as an index of quality;
but supposing the sample when first drawn to be fair, in the
very act of drawing, and at every subsequent examination it is
liable to lose some of the sand which it contains, and very
shortly to become nothing better than 'a delusion, a mockery,
and a snare.'

"This sandy adulteration, too, is more difficult to deal with than the simpler one before mentioned : when stones are found in cotton bales it is at once evident that they have no business there; they were not represented in the sample, and were, therefore, not expected, consequently an affidavit is made of their presence, and a claim for compensation is preferred.   It is true that a spinner has occasionally suffered the inconvenience of having his mill burned down, in consequence of contact between a flint and the iron machinery ; but as this is not of *very* frequent occurrence, it may, perhaps, be taken out of the account.

"But as regards sand, which is nominally, if not actually or fairly represented in the sample, it is plain that if the spinner make a claim on this score, he is liable to be told that the price he paid was calculated upon the fact of the presence of this sand, and that it would be a point of no small difficulty to settle such a claim equitably if allowed at all.   No wonder, therefore, that there are so many bales of cotton at Liverpool which manufacturers decline to touch.

"The money actually paid to America for this stuff does not represent the extent of the evil ; freight, warehouse rent, and other charges are all incurred on this mass of useless earth, just as though it were what it ought to be ; to say nothing of the damage caused to machinery, and the detriment to the health of the work-people in factories where the adulterated cotton is used.

"This fraud has assumed such proportions that active steps are taken for its abatement.   It is clear that the check must ultimately come from the consumer, for as long as a market exists for such cotton, so long will people be found to supply it.   Whatever may be the result of the means adopted with a view to the suppression of this gigantic swindle, it cannot be denied that its perpetration is a strong argument against our remaining longer than can be avoided, dependent upon one country for the largest supply of so important an article as cotton.

"It is stated by those whose assertions are worthy of respect, that cotton could be grown in Africa, and laid down in England at considerably lower prices—quality for quality—than that brought from New Orleans.   No doubt time and capital are requisite to render Africa to any extent available as a source of

supply ; but most certainly £2,000,000 sterling might have been far better spent in this direction during the past year, than in paying for an enormous quantity of useless and mischievous rubbish, and in thus helping to encourage and support a shameful and systematic fraud."—C. P. WILLIAM.

CHAPTER X.

THE DANGER OF THE SOUTH.

"BEFORE the advent of modern science, any idea of systematic laws of human improvement would have been deemed alike impossible and absurd; but the constant observation of facts, the exact statistics recorded, the progress of science in all departments, has made it possible to conceive of, and probable that there actually exist *uniform laws of social movements*, based upon any given condition of society. If the *elementary social* condition be different in regard to religion, government, arts, science, industry, the resulting movements of society will be different. Hence, when we have ascertained by accurate observation upon, and record of, the social phenomena, that the social movement is uniformly in a certain direction, and that certain results uniformly follow, we shall know in what *elements* the conditions of society must be changed, in order to change the results. Hence, when this law of social movements is ascertained, the philanthropist, legislator, and jurist will know precisely what must be done, and how in order to remove the evils, or reform the wrongs, or produce the results they desire. They will know that *certain elementary conditions of society* must be changed, and they well know that by removing temptations, or laying restraints, or enlightening the mind, or changing the course of industry, or producing new arts, they will change the social tendency, and thus change the results. * * * Society, or that part of it which thinks and acts, can change the results by changing the elementary conditions which produce them. When you know exactly what the change ought to be, it is not very difficult to produce it; nor does it follow that because a thousand crimes must be committed in Ohio, that a thousand particular individuals *must* commit them. It is true that the individual frequently acts from motives, but is it not just as true

213

that the individual frequently seeks these motives, and presents
them to himself."—From the *Report of the Ohio State Commissioner of Statistics*, 1859.

"If there is a first principle in intellectual education it is this
that the discipline which does good to the mind is that in which
the mind is active, not that in which it is passive. The secret
for developing the faculties is to give them much to do, and
much inducement to do it."—MILL's *Political Economy*.

The field-hand negro is, on an average, a very poor
and very bad creature, much worse than I had supposed
before I had seen him and grown familiar with his
stupidity, indolence, duplicity, and sensuality. He
seems to be but an imperfect man, incapable of taking
care of himself in a civilized manner, and his presence
in large numbers must be considered a dangerous circumstance to a civilized people.

A civilized people, within which a large number of
such creatures has been placed by any means not within
its own control, has claims upon the charity, the aid, if
necessary, of all other civilized peoples in its endeavors
to relieve itself from the danger which must be apprehended from their brutal propensities, from the incom-
pleteness of their human sympathies—their inhumanity
—from their natural love of ease, and the barbaric want
of forethought and providence, which would often induce desperate want among them. Evidently the
people thus burdened would have need to provide
systematically for the physical wants of these poor
creatures, else the latter would be liable to prey with
great waste upon their substance. Perhaps the very
best thing to do would be to collect them into small

herds, and attach each herd to a civilized family, the
head of which should be responsible for its safe keeping. Such a superintendent should of course contrive,
if possible, to make his herd contribute in some
way to the procuring of its necessary sustenance; and
if, besides this, he even turned their feeble abilities
to such good account by his superior judgment, that
they actually procured a considerable surplus of
food and clothing for the benefit of others, should not
Christendom applaud and encourage his exertions,
even if a certain amount of severity and physical con-
straint had been found necessary to accomplish this
success?

Let us endeavor to assume a similar difficulty for ourselves. Let us suppose that a large part—the proportion
varying with the locality—of our own community should
next year suffer from some new malady, the result of
which should in no case be fatal, but which should, like
the *goitre* of Savoy, leave all who were affected by it
permanently injured in their intellects, with diminished
bodily activity, and fiercer animal propensities. (I take
this method of stating the case, because some of us who
only see the negro as he exists at the North might find
it difficult to imagine him as he is known to the
planters.)

Suppose, further, that this malady should be confined
to certain families, as if its seed had been received hundreds of years ago by numerous individuals, and only
their descendants (but all of these to the most distant
trace of the blood), now suffered from it. Also, that

some of our doctors should be of the opinion that the effects of the malady upon the intellect would descend to the children, and to all descendants of those who suffered.   Suppose that these unfortunates should be subject to certain hallucinations, that they should be liable to think themselves sane and quite able to take care of themselves, and that when possessed with these ideas that they should be quite cunning and dangerous in attempting to exercise the usual prerogatives of sane men.

What should we do with them?

Finding them ordinarily tractable and sensible enough, after all, to yield readily, if not cheerfully, to superior force, we might herd them together on a sort of farm-hospitals, and let them earn their living, giving especially capable men charge of many, and rewarding them with good salaries, and ordinary small farmers, smaller numbers, with smaller compensations for overseeing them?

Of course, we should place every possible legislative guard and check upon these superintendents and overseers to secure fair and honest dealing, to prevent them from making perquisites for themselves at the expense of a reasonable comfort in their institutions.   Careful instructions to secure economical sustenance, and how to turn such labor as could be got from the unfortunates to the best account, in defraying the cost of their keeping, would also be framed by talented men and furnished each keeper.

And having regard to national wealth, to the tem-

poral good of the commonwealth, this is about all that
common sense would lead us to do, at least through the
agency of government.

Is this all, reader?

You have too much overlooked our small matters of
State, if you think so.   We have a few crazy people, a
few fools, not enough to be a matter of much consideration to our statesmen or legislators, yet we have a
State system in our dealing with them, such as it is,
and such as it is, it puts our dealing with them on a
little different footing than would the system I have
above imagined.   What I have imagined is not quite
all we have for some time been in the habit of doing
when we did anything with this class.   And judging
from what we have done, it does not seem as if it would
be all that we should do in such an emergency as I have
supposed, engaging as it would all the talent of the
country to diminish as much as possible the necessary
results of the calamity.

We should, it appears, call upon our learned doctors
eagerly to study; we should each of us eagerly observe
for ourselves whether the fearful infirmity by which so
many were incapacitated for their former usefulness,
were not only absolutely incurable, but also absolutely
not possible to be alleviated.   And if our observation
should satisfy us, if our doctors could not deny that, with
judicious treatment, a considerable alleviation could
be effected, so much so indeed, that with a very large
part a close approximation to the normal condition of
sane and capable mankind could be obtained, there are

doubtless those amongst us who would think this a
dangerous and an infidel presumption. Just as every
year some miserable wretch is found in our dark places
to have a crazy father or brother whom he keeps in a
cage in his garret, and whose estate he takes care of,
and who is of the opinion that it will be of no use, but,
on the contrary, a manifest defiance of Divine Providence, and most dangerous to life and property to let
this unfortunate out of his cage, to surround him with
comforts, and contrive for him cheerful occupation, as
our State requires shall be done. But would the average
common sense and humanity of the people of the Free
States allow them to refuse all reduction from their usual
annual incomes; refuse to suffer all necessary addition
to their usual taxes; refuse to burden their minds with
the difficulties of the all-absorbing problem, in order to
initiate a remedial system? Our worst and most cow-
ardly legislature would never dare adjourn leaving his
duty incompletely performed. There are thousands on
thousands of our citizens who would not only spare from
their incomes, but would divide their estates for such a
purpose. There is not a county that would not submit
to the highest war taxes for it.

Suppose that the doctors and that the universal observation of the community should determine that the
defective class were not only capable of being improved,
but that so far as their limited intellects permitted, the
laws of improvement were the same for them as for
healthy men; that they were found to be influenced by a
liking for food and drink, for the society of each other

and of sane men, for the admiration and respect of each
other and of sane men, for their ease, for dancing, for
music, and other amusements; and that their imperfect
natures could be acted upon, drawn out, and enlarged by
means of these likings.   Suppose that it were found that
nearly all of them had still some knowledge of religion,
that although they were inclined sometimes to consider
sane men as their enemies, they were still, in most cases,
by judicious play upon their inclinations and disinclina-
tions, capable of being trained quite beyond the most
sagacious of our domestic animals, even to read intelligently.   Should we, because there were so many of
them, go back two hundred years in our civilization,
denying ourselves the addition which this capacity
would give to their powers of usefulness, and consequently of economy of maintenance; denying them the
advantages for improvement which we now in every
State give to our hopelessly insane, to our blind and
mute, to our fools, to our worst and most dangerous
criminals?

Why do we not pass laws forbidding criminals and
maniacs to read?   Our fathers did not allow them to
read when negroes were introduced in Virginia.   But
every man among us whom we call well informed, now
knows that it is a profitable business for the State,
which has so little profitable business, even to provide
teachers and books for a portion of her criminals, to
allow books and encourage reading with all.   To provide books, to provide physicians, to provide teachers,
to provide halls and gardens of recreation, as stimulants

to healthful thought for our madmen and our fools; to
this the State is impelled equally by considerations of
safety and of economy. Even Kentucky has its State institution for the development of manhood in fools born
of white women.

Does not every such man know, too, that given an im-
provable mind with a sound body, possessed of the natural instincts, the usual desires, appetites, aversions, no
matter if, at starting, the being is even what we call an
idiot, a drivelling imbecile, disgusting all who see him,
a sheer burden upon society, the process of making him
clean in his habits, capable of laboring with a good and
intelligent purpose, and of associating inoffensively
with others, is just as certain in its principles and in
its progress—infinite progress—as the navigation of a
ship or the building of a house?

This is even so with a cretin, whose body is deformed
beyond remedy, whose brain is contracted, whose face
is contorted, whose limbs are half paralyzed, whose
every organ is defective, and who has inherited these
conditions from goitrous parents and grandparents.

Dr. Seguin says: "The idiot wishes for nothing; he
wishes only to remain in his vacuity."

Even so thinks Dr. Cartwright of the negro, and
surely nothing worse can be thought of him.[1]

But Dr. Seguin adds : "To treat successfully this ill-

[1] "The negro, docile in subjection, attached like the household dog to his master, only in proportion to his intellect, in a
far higher grade of being, is satisfied and happy in the half-
civilized condition which, with us, his *imitativeness* enables
him to attain."—De Bow's *Resources*, vol. ii., p. 203.

will [indisposition to take care of himself], the physician wills that the idiot should act *and think himself, of himself, and finally, by himself.* The incessant volition of the moral physician urges incessantly the idiot into the sphere of activity, of thinking, of labor, of duty, and affectionate feelings.''

Is there no such law of progression of capacity for the black imbeciles? All the laws of the South have the contrary aims ; to withdraw them as much as possible from the sphere of self-willed activity, thought, labor—to prevent the negro from thinking by himself, of himself, for himself ; and the principle on which these laws are based is thus defined by Mr. De Bow :

" The Almighty has thought well to place certain of His creatures in certain *fixed positions* in this world of ours, for what cause He has not seen fit to make quite clear to our limited capacities ; and why an ass is not a man, and a man is not an ass, will probably forever remain a mystery." "God made the world ; God gave thee thy place, my hirsute brother, and according to all earthly possibilities, and probabilities it is thy destiny there to remain, bray as thou wilt. From the same great power have our sable friends, Messrs. Sambo, Cuffee & Co., received their position also. * * * Alas, my poor black brother, thou, like thy hirsute friend, must do thy braying in vain. " [1]

Are there laws on our statute books to prevent asses from being taught to read?

The Richmond *Examiner* says :

" These immigrants do not, like our ancestors, fly from religous and political persecution ; they come merely as animals in search of a richer and fresher pasture. They come to gratify physical want—for moral, intellectual, or religious wants they

---

[1] *Resources*, vol. ii., pp. 197, 198.

have not acquired. They will settle in large masses, and, for ages to come, will practise and inculcate a pure (or rather impure) materialism. Mormonism is a fit exponent, proof, and illustration of our theory. The mass of them are sensual, grovelling, low-minded agrarians, and nine tenths of them would join the Mormons, or some such brutal, levelling sect, if an opportunity offered to do so.

"European writers describe a large class of population throughout England and the Continent as being distinguished by restless, wandering, nomadic habits, and by a peculiar conformation of the skull and face. Animal and sensual nature largely predominates, with them, over the moral and intellectual. It is they who commit crimes, fill prisons, and adorn the gallows. They will not submit to the restraints of law or religion, nor can they be educated. From their restless and lawless habits, we should infer they composed a large part of the Northern immigration."

If all this were true, and were felt by us to be true, should we think it necessary to put the minds of these beings in fetters? Should we hold it to be dangerous if one should undertake to strengthen their intellects, to give them larger ideas?

If all the slaves in the United States were "real Congo niggers," which not one in one thousand is, and if all real Congo niggers were as incapable, and as beastly, and as savage in their propensities as the very worst of them are asserted to be, would the method of dealing with them which the legislature of the Slave States, and which a large part of the labor of the Congress and Executive of our confederation is directed to the purpose of perpetuating, be felt to be strictly in accordance with sound and well established economico-political principles? The purpose of that legislation is avowed to be merely to secure safety with economy. Would a pro-

ject for establishing an institution planned upon the
principles of the ancient Bedlam and the ancient Bride-
well be felt to-day to be completely justified among
us, by the statement that highwaymen and maniacs
will endanger life and the security of our property if
they are not somehow taken care of?

If there had been no Mettray with its Demetz, no
Norfolk Island with its Machonochie, no Hanwell with
its Connolly, no Abendberg with its Guggenbuhl; if
the courage, devotion, and labor of Pinel, Sicard, and
Seguin had been in vain; if there had been no progress in the science of civilized society since the days of
Howard, we might listen with merely silent sadness to
such an excuse for debilitating the weak, for holding
down the fallen; for permitting brutal keepers to exas-
perate the mad and mercenary nurses to stupefy the
idiotic; we might, if we saw it to be necessary to pre-
serve a civilized community from destruction, even give
its object our aid, but with the knowledge which in our
time is every where else acted upon, it is impossible for
us not to feel that such an argument is a specious and
a fallacious one, and that no State can long act upon it
with safety, much less with economy.

And surely the system by which intellectual demands
and ambitions are repressed in the negro is as little calculated to produce the security which is its object, as it
is to turn his physical abilities to the most profitable
use for his owner.   How far it fails in this respect, the
extra legal measure, of safety and the semi-instinct-
ive habits of unconscious precaution which pervade

Southern society evince. I say unconscious precaution, because Southerners themselves seem to have generally a very inadequate idea of the influence of slavery upon their habits in this way, and this is very natural.

Every habit breeds unconsciousness of its existence in the mind of the man whom it controls, and this is more true of habits which involve our safety than of any others. The weary sailor aloft, on the lookout, may fall asleep ; but, in the lurch of the ship, his hands will clench the swaying cordage only the more firmly, that they act in the method of instinct. A hard-hunted fugitive may nod in his saddle, but his knees will not unloose their hold upon his horse. Men who live in powder-mills are said to lose all conscious feeling of habitual insecurity ; but visitors perceive that they have acquired a constant softness of manner and of voice.

If a laborer on a plantation should insolently contradict his master, it may often appear to be no more than a reasonable precaution for his master to kill him on the spot ; for when a slave has acquired such boldness, it may be evident that not merely is his value as property seriously diminished, but that the attempt to make further use of him at all, as property, involves in danger the whole white community. " If I let this man live, and permit him the necessary degree of freedom to be further useful to me, he will infect with his audacity all my negro property, which will be correspondingly more difficult to control, and correspondingly reduced in value. If he treats me with so little respect now, what

have I to anticipate when he has found other equally independent spirits among the slaves? They will not alone make themselves free, but will avenge upon me, and my wife, and my daughters, and upon all our community, the injustice which they will think has been done them, and their women, and children.'' Thus would he reason, and shudder to think what might follow if he yielded to an impulse of mercy.

To suppose, however, that the master will pause while he thus weighs the danger exactly, and then deliberately act as, upon reflection, he considers the necessities of the case demand, is absurd. The mere circumstance of his doing so would nourish a hopeful spirit in the slave, and stimulate him to consider how he could best avoid all punishment. Hence the instinct-like habit of precaution with individuals, and hence the frenzy which often seizes whole communities.

But, ''planters sleep unguarded, and with their bed-room doors open.'' So, as it was boasted, did the Emperor at Biarritz, last summer, and with greater bravery, because the assassin of Napoleon would be more sure, in dispatching him, that there would be no one left with a vital interest to secure punishment for such a deed : and because, if he failed, Napoleon dare never employ such exemplary punishment for his enemies as would the planters for theirs. The emperors of the South are the whole free society of the South, and it is a society of mutual assurance. Against a slave who has the disposition to become an assassin, his emperor has a body-guard, which, for general effectiveness, is to the Cent

Garde as your right hand is to your right hand's glove.

It is but a few months since, in Georgia or Alabama, a man treated another precisely as Mr. Brooks treated Mr. Sumner—coming up behind him, with the fury of a madman, and felling him with a bludgeon ; killing him by the first blow, however, and then discharging vengeance by repeated strokes upon his senseless body.[1] The man thus pitifully abused had been the master of the other, a remarkably confiding and merciful master, it was said—too much so ; " It never does to be too slack with niggers." By such indiscretion he

---

[1] The late Mr. Brooks' character should be honestly considered, now that personal enmity toward him is impossible. That he was courteous, accomplished, warm-hearted, and hot-blooded, dear as a friend and fearful as an enemy, may be believed by all ; but, in the South, his name is yet never mentioned without the term gallant or courageous, spirited or noble, being also attached to it, and we are obliged to ask, why insist on this ? The truth is, we include a habit of mind in these terms which slavery has rendered, in a great degree, obsolete in the South. The man who has been accustomed from childhood to see men beaten when they have no chance to defend themselves ; to hear men accused, reproved, and vituperated, who dare not open their lips in self-defence or reply ; the man who is accustomed to see other men whip women without interference, remonstrance, or any expression of indignation, must have a certain quality, which is an essential part of personal honor with us, greatly blunted, if not entirely destroyed. The same quality which we detest in the assassination of an enemy, is essentially constant in all slavery. It is found in effecting one's will with another, when he cannot, if he would, defend himself. Accustomed to this in every hour of their lives Southerners do not feel magnanimity and the " fair-play " impulse to be a necessary part of the quality of " spirit," courage, and nobleness. By spirit they apparently mean only passionate vindictiveness of character, and by gallantry mere intrepidity.

brought his death upon him. But did his assassin escape? He was roasted, at a slow fire, on the spot of the murder, in the presence of many thousand slaves, driven to the ground from all the adjoining counties, and when, at length, his life went out, the fire was intensified until his body was in ashes, which were scattered to the winds and trampled under foot. Then "magistrates and clergymen" addressed appropriate warnings to the assembled subjects. It was not thought indiscreet to leave doors open again that night.

Will any traveller say that he has seen no signs of discontent, or insecurity, or apprehension, or precaution ; that the South has appeared quieter and less excited, even on the subject of slavery, than the North ; that the negroes seem happy and contented, and the citizens more tranquilly engaged in the pursuit of their business and pleasure ? Has that traveller been in Naples? Precisely the same remarks apply to the appearance of things there at this moment. The massacre of Hayti opened in a ball-room. Mr. Cobden judged there was not the smallest reason in the French king's surrounding himself with soldiers the day before the hidden force of insubordination broke forth and cast him forth from his kingdom. It is true, however, that the tranquillity of the South is the tranquillity of Hungary and of Poland, rather than of France or the Two Sicilies ; the tranquillity of hopelessness on the part of the subject race. But, in the most favored regions, this broken spirit of despair is as carefully preserved by the citizens, and with as confident and unhesitating an ap-

plication of force, when necessary to teach humility, as it is by the army of the Czar, or the omnipresent police of the Kaiser. In Richmond, and Charleston, and New Orleans, the citizens are as careless and gay as in Boston or London, and their servants a thousand times as child-like and cordial, to all appearance, in their relations with them as our servants are with us. But go to the bottom of this security and dependence, and you come to police machinery such as you never find in towns under free government ; citadels, sentries, passports, grape-shotted cannon, and daily public whippings of the subjects for accidental infractions of police ceremonies. I happened myself to see more direct expression of tyranny in a single day and night at Charleston, than at Naples in a week ; and I found that more than half the inhabitants of this town were subject to arrest, imprisonment, and barbarous punishment, if found in the streets without a passport after the evening "gunfire." Similar precautions and similar customs may be discovered in every large town in the South.

Nor is it so much better, as is generally imagined, in the rural districts. Ordinarily there is no show of government any more than at the North : the slaves go about with as much apparent freedom as convicts in a dockyard. There is, however, nearly everywhere, always prepared to act, if not always in service, an armed force, with a military organization, which is invested with more arbitrary and cruel power than any police in Europe. Yet the security of the whites is in a much less

degree contingent on the action of the patrols than upon the constant, habitual, and instinctive surveillance and authority of all white people over all black. I have seen a gentleman, with no commission or special authority, oblige negroes to show their passports, simply because he did not recognize them as belonging to any of his neighbors. I have seen a girl, twelve years old, in a district where, in ten miles, the slave population was fifty to one of the free, stop an old man on the public road, demand to know where he was going, and by what authority, order him to face about and return to his plantation, and enforce her command with turbulent anger, when he hesitated, by threatening that she would have him well whipped if he did not instantly obey. The man quailed like a spaniel, and she instantly resumed the manner of a lovely child with me, no more apprehending that she had acted unbecomingly, than that her character had been influenced by the slave's submission to her caprice of supremacy; no more conscious that she had increased the security of her life by strengthening the habit of the slave to the master race, than is the sleeping seaman that he tightens his clutch of the rigging as the ship meets each new billow.

There is no part of the South in which the people are more free from the direct action of slavery upon the character, or where they have less to apprehend from rebellion, than Eastern Tennessee. Yet after the burning of a negro near Knoxville, a few years ago, the deed was justified as necessary for the maintenance of order among the slaves, by the editor of a newspaper (the

Register) which, owing to its peculiarly conservative character, I have heard stigmatized as "an abolition print." "It was," he observed, "a means of absolute, necessary self-defence, which could not be secured by an ordinary resort to the laws. Two executions on the gallows have occurred in this county within a year or two past, and the example has been unavailing. Four executions by hanging have taken place, heretofore, in Jefferson, of slaves guilty of similar offences, and it has produced no radical terror or example for the others designing the same crimes, and hence any example less horrible and terrifying would have availed nothing here."

The other local paper (the *Whig*), upon the same occasion, used the following language :

"We have to say in defence of the act, that it was not perpetrated by an excited multitude, but by one thousand citizens—good citizens at that—who were cool, calm, and deliberate."

And the editor, who is a Methodist preacher, presently adds, after explaining the enormity of the offence with which the victim was charged—"We unhesitatingly affirm that the punishment was unequal to the crime. Had we been there we should have taken a part, and even suggested the pinching of pieces out of him with red-hot pincers—the cutting off of a limb at a time, and then burning them all in a heap. The possibility of his escaping from jail forbids the idea of awaiting the tardy movements of the law." [Although one thousand trusty citizens volunteered to guard him at the stake.]

How much more horrible than the deed are these
apologies for it. They make it manifest that it was not
accidental in its character, but a phenomenon of general
and fundamental significance. They explain the para-
lytic effect upon the popular conscience of the great
calamity of the South. They indicate a necessary
tendency of people living under such circumstances to
return in their habits of thought to the dark ages of
mankind. For who, from the outside, can fail to see
that the real reason why men in the middle of the nineteenth century, and in the center of the United States,
are publicly burned at the stake is one much less
heathenish, less disgraceful to the citizens than that
given by the more zealous and extemporaneous of their
journalistic exponents—the desire to torture the sinner
proportionately to the measure of his sin. Doubtless,
this reverend gentleman expresses the uppermost feeling of the ruling mind of his community. But would
a similar provocation have developed a similar aveng-
ing spirit in any other nominally Christian or civilized
people? Certainly not. All over Europe, and in every
Free State—California, for significant reasons, temporarily excepted—in similar cases, justice deliberately
takes its course; the accused is systematically assisted
in defending or excusing himself. If the law demands
his life, the infliction of unnecessary suffering, and the
education of the people in violence and feelings of re-
venge, is studiously avoided. Go back to the foundation of the custom which thus neutralizes Christianity
among the people of the South, which carries them back-

ward blindly against the tide of civilization, and what do
we find it to be? The editor who still retains moral
health enough to be suspected—as men more enlightened
than their neighbors usually are—of heterodoxy, an-
swers. To follow the usual customs of civilization elsewhere would not be felt safe. To indulge in feelings
of humanity would not be felt safe. To be faithful to
the precepts of Christ would not be felt safe. To act
in a spirit of cruel, inconsiderate, illegal, violent, and
pitiless vengeance, must be permitted, must be counten-
anced, must be defended by the most conservative, as
a "means of absolute, necessary self-defence." To educate the people practically otherwise would be felt to be
suicidal. Hence no free press, no free pulpit, no free
politics can be permitted in the South. Hence every
white stripling in the South may carry a dirk-knife in his
pocket, and play with a revolver before he has learned
to swim.[1]

I happened to pass through Eastern Tennessee shortly
after this tragedy, and conversed with a man who was
engaged in it—a mild, common-sense native of the country. He told me that there was no evidence against the
negro but his own confession. I suggested that he might
have been crazy. " What if he was?" he asked, with
a sudden asperity. What if he was, to be sure? The
slaves who were brought together to witness his torture
were not insane. They were at least capable of instruction. That day they were given a lesson; were taught
to know their masters better; were taught that when

[1] From the Introduction to *The Englishman in Kansas*.

ordinary and legal discipline failed, resort would be had
to more potent means of governing them.   A better
informed man, having regard to the ignorance of a
stranger, might have answered me : " It was of no
consequence, practically, whether he were sane or mad.
We do not wish our slaves to study the right and the
wrong of every exciting occurrence.   To say that being
mad the negro was not responsible, therefore not guilty
of a crime, therefore not to be punished, would be proclaiming to them that only that which is wrong is to be
dreaded.   Whatever offends us, whatever is against our
will and pleasure, is what a slave must be made to
dread."

Constantly, and everywhere throughout the South,
are there occurrences of this significance.   I do not say
as horrible, though no year in the last ten has passed
without something as bad—but, constantly and everywhere, of the same nature, of the same impulse, the
same reasoning, the same purposes, the same disregard
of principles of society, which no people can ever set
aside and not have reason to feel their situation insecure.
It is false, it is the most dangerous mistake possible to
assume that this feeling of insecurity, this annihilation
of the only possible basis of security in human society,
is, in the slightest degree, the result of modern agitation.
It is the fundamental law of slavery, as distinctly appears in the decision of Justice Ruffin, of North Carolina,
in the case of the State *vs.* Mann.[1]   The American system of slavery from its earliest years (as shown in

[1] Devereaux's *North Carolina Reports*, 263.

Seaboard Slave States),[1] and without cessation to
the present time, has had this accompaniment. Less
in the last twenty years, if anything, than before.
Would it not be more just to say that this element of
the present system was the cause of agitation? Must
not the determined policy of the South to deal with
slavery on the assumption that it is, in its present form,
necessary, just, good, and to be extended, strengthened,
and perpetuated indefinitely, involve constant agitation
as a necessary incident of the means used to carry it out?
I do not say with you or with me, reader, but with a
goodly number of any civilized community? Do you
not, who wish to think otherwise, consider that it will
always require what you must deem a superior mind
not to be overcome by incidents necessary to the carrying out of this determination? And will not such
agitation give renewed sense of danger, and occasion
renewed demands for assurance from us?

I have remarked before that in no single instance did
I find an inquiry of the owner or the overseer of a large
plantation about the poor whites of its vicinity fail to
elicit an expression indicating habitual irritation with
them. This equally with the polished and tranquil
gentleman of South Carolina and the rude pioneer
settler of Texas, himself born a dirt-eating sand-hiller.
It was evident in most cases, and in one it was distinctly
explained to me by a Louisianian planter (as narrated
in *Seaboard Slave States*),[2] that the reason of this
was not merely the bad effect upon the discipline of

[1] Vol. ii., p. 132.   [2] Vol. ii., p. 333.

the plantation, which was had by the intercourse between these people and the slaves, but that it was felt
that the contrast between the habits of the former—
most of the time idle, and when working, working only
for their own benefit and without a master—constantly
offered suggestions and temptations to the slaves to
neglect their duty, to run away and live a vagabond
life, as these poor whites were seen to.   Hence, one of
the acknowledged advantages of very large and isolated
plantations, and hence, in part, the desire of every
planter to get possession of the land of any poor non-
slaveholding neighbor.

As few Southern writers seem to have noticed this, I
suppose that few Southerners are aware how universal
with planters is this feeling.   My attention being early
directed to the causes of the condition of the poor whites,
I never failed to make inquiries of planters, and of intelligent men especially, about those in their neighborhood, and being soon struck by the constant recurrence
of similar expressions with regard to them, I was the
more careful to introduce the subject at every proper
opportunity, and, I repeat, always with the same result.   I am afraid that the feeling of the South to the
North is (more or less defined in individual minds) of
the same nature, and that the contiguity of a people
whose laborers take care of themselves, and labor industriously without being owned—that intimate relations and intercourse with such a people can never be
felt to be safe by slaveholders.   That it must always be
looked upon with apprehension, with a sense of danger,

more or less vague, more or less well defined, but always sufficient to lead to efforts intended to counteract its natural influence—its influence not so much with slaves, certainly not alone with the slaves, but also with that important element of population which reaps no profit from the good behavior of the slaves.

In De Bow's *Review* for January, 1850, will be found the following passage in an article discussing the practicability of employing the non-slaveholding whites in factories, the argument being that there will be less danger of their becoming "abolitionists" under such circumstances than at present exists:

"The great mass of our poor white population begin to understand that they have rights, and that they, too, are entitled to some of the sympathy which falls upon the suffering. They are fast learning that there is an almost infinite world of industry opening before them by which they can elevate themselves and their families from wretchedness and ignorance to competence and intelligence. It is this great upheaving of our masses that we have to fear, so far as our institutions are concerned."

It is, in the nature of things, while slaveholders refuse the slightest concession to the spirit of the age—while, in their legislation, they refuse to recognize, in the slightest degree, the principles of social science under which we live and must live, and which every civilized people has fully adopted, that they should endeavor to make it appear the fault of others that they do not feel assured of safety and at ease with themselves; that they should try to make their own ignorant people believe that it is from without all danger is to be apprehended—all assurance of safety to be

clamored for—that they should endeavor to make
themselves believe it.[1]

Those who seriously propose to stop all agitation on
the subject of slavery, by causing the abolitionists to
refrain from proceedings which cause apprehension at
the South, by silencing all who entertain sentiments
the utterance of which is deemed a source of "danger
to Southern institutions," by refraining themselves from
all proceedings which will be looked upon with alarm
by their fellow-citizens of the Slave States, can know
very little of what would be required before the South
were satisfied. The destruction of some million dollars'
cost in school and text-books would be one of the first
and yet a small item in the undertaking. Books which
directly comment upon slavery are considered comparatively safe by those who think that they comprehend
the situation of the South, because their purpose being
defined, they can be guarded against. As is well understood, it is the insidious attacks of a free press that
are most feared. But is it well understood what are

[1] The real object of the systematic mail robbery which is
maintained throughout the South, and of the censorship of the
press which is otherwise attempted, was once betrayed by a
somewhat disgusting Southern editor, Duff Green, in the
United States Telegraph, in the following words :

"The real danger of this [slave insurrection] is remote. We
believe we have most to fear from the organized action upon
the consciences and fears of the slaveholders themselves ; from
the insinuation of their dangerous heresies into our schools, our
pulpits, and our domestic circles. It is only by alarming the
consciences of the weak and feeble, and diffusing among our
people a morbid sensibility on the question of slavery, that the
abolitionists can accomplish their object."

felt to be "insidious attacks?" Some idea may be
formed from the following passages which I take, not
from the heated columns of a daily newspaper, but
from the cool pages of the deliberate *De Bow's Review*.
The apprehension they express is not of to-day ; in the
first article from which I quote (which was published
in the middle of Mr. Pierce's presidential term) reference is made to warnings of the same character which
have been sounded from time to time before ; and this
very number of the *Review* contains a testimonial from
fifty-five Southern senators and representatives in Congress to the "ability and accuracy" of its "exposition
of the working of the system of polity of the Southern
States."

"Our text-books are abolition books. They are so to the extent of their capacity." * * * "We have been too careless
and indifferent to the import of these things."

"And so long as we use such works as *Wayland's Moral
Science*, and the abolition geographies, readers, and histories,
overrunning, as they do, with all sorts of slanders, caricatures,
and blood-thirsty sentiments, let us never complain of their
[Northern Church people's] use of that transitory romance
[*Uncle Tom's Cabin*]. They seek to array our children, by
false ideas, against the established ordinance of God ; and it
sometimes takes effect. A professor in one of our Southern
seminaries, not long since, placed in the hands of a pupil *Wayland's Moral Science*, and informed her that the chapter on
slavery was heretical and unscriptural, and that she would not be
examined on that chapter, and need not study it. *Perhaps* she
did n't. But on the day of examination she wished her teacher
to tell her 'if that chapter was heretical how she was to know
but they were all so?' We might enumerate many other books
of similar character and tendencies. But we will refer to only
one more—it is *Gilbert's Atlas*—though the real author's name
does not appear on the title page. On the title page it is

called *Appleton's Complete Guide of the World;* published by
D. Appleton & Co., New York. This is an elegant and com-
prehensive volume, endorsed by the Appletons and sent South,
containing hidden lessons of the most fiendish and murderous
character that enraged fanaticism could conceive or indite.
It is a sort of literary and scientific infernal machine. And
whatever the design may have been, the tendency is as shocking as the imagination can picture.[1] * * * This is the ar-
tillery and these the implements England and our own recre-
ant sister States are employing to overturn the order of society
and the established forms of labor that date back beyond the
penning of the Decalogue. * * * This book, and many
other Northern school books scattered over the country, come
within the range of the statutes of this State, which provide
for the imprisonment for life or the infliction of the penalty
of death upon any person who shall 'publish or distribute' such
works ; and were I a citizen of New Orleans, this work should
not escape the attention of the grand jury. But need I add
more to convince the skeptical of the necessity there is for
the production of our own text-books, and, may I not add, our
own literature? Why should the land of domestic servitude be
less productive in the great works of the mind now than when
Homer evoked the arts, poetry, and eloquence into existence?
Moses wrote the Genesis of Creation, the Exodus of Israel, and
the laws of mankind? and when Cicero, Virgil, Horace, St.
John, and St. Paul became the instructors of the world?[2]
* * * They will want no cut-throat literature, no fire-brand
moral science * * * nor Appleton's *Complete Atlas*, to encourage crimes that would blanch the cheek of a pirate, nor any
of the ulcerous and polluting agencies issuing from the hot-beds
of abolition fanaticism."

From an article on educational reform at the South,

[1] Elsewhere the Messrs. Appleton are spoken of as "THE
GREAT ABOLITION PUBLISHERS OF NEW YORK."

[2] Note the argument, I pray you, reader. Why, indeed?
Why is there not a Feejee Iliad? Are not the Feejees heathen,
as Homer was? Why should not the Book of Mormon be as
good a thing as the Psalms of David? Was not Joseph Smith
also a polygamist?

in the same *Review*, 1856, I take the following indications of what, among other Northern doings, are considered to imperil the South :

"*Lovell's United States Speaker*, the *National Reader*, the *Young Ladies' Reader*, *Columbian Orator*, *Scott's Lessons*, the *Village Reader*, and numerous others, have been used for years, and are all, in some respects, valuable compilations. We apprehend, however, there are few parents or teachers who are familiar with the whole of their contents, or they would demand expurgated editions for the use of their children. The sickly sentimentality of the poet Cowper, whose ear became so 'pained,' and his soul 'sick with every day's report of wrong and outrage,' that it made him cry out in agony for 'a lodge in some vast wilderness,' where he might commune with howling wolves and panthers on the blessings of *liberty* (?), stamps its infectious poison upon many of the pages of these works." * * *

"From the *American First Class Book*, page 185, we quote another more modern sentiment, which bears no less higher authority than the name of the great Massachusetts statesman, Mr. Webster."

Having burnt or expurgated Webster and Cowper, is it to be imagined that the leaders of opinion in the South would yet be willing to permit familiar intercourse between themselves and a people who allowed a book containing such lines as these to circulate freely :

> "What is a man
> If his chief good and market of his time
> Be but to sleep and feed?   A beast, no more.
> Sure, He that made us with such large discourse,
> Looking before and after, gave us not
> That capability and Godlike reason,
> To rust unused."

What a dangerous sentiment to come by any chance

to a slave! Is it not? Are you, then, prepared to burn your Shakespeare? I will not ask if you will have another book "expurgated" of all passages the tendency of which is to set the bondmen free.

If the security of life and property at the South must for ever be dependent on the thoroughness with which the negro population is prevented from acquiring knowledge, from thinking of themselves and for themselves, it will never be felt to be greater than it is to-day. Efforts made to increase this security will of themselves occasion agitation, and agitation must counteract those efforts. Knowledge, knowledge of what is going on elsewhere, of the condition of men elsewhere, of what is thought elsewhere, must have increased currency with every class of mankind in all parts of this continent, as it increases in population, and the movements of its population increase in activity and importance. No human laws, embargoes, or armies and navies can prevent it. Do our utmost, we cannot go back of the steam-engine, the telegraph, the cotton-gin, and the cylinder-press. The South has admitted steamboats and railroads. It was not practicable to stop with these, and bar out all the rest that is peculiar to the nineteenth century. Is it practicable to admit the machinery of modern civilized life, and not stir up its free people? Is it practicable to stir up its intermediate class, and keep its lowest torpid? Assuredly the security which depends upon preventing either of these steps can never be permanently increased ; spite of all possible further extension of slave territory, and disper-

sion and disconnection of plantations, it must gradually lessen. As it lessens, the demand upon the nation to supply new grounds of security must increase—increase continually, until at length, this year, next year, or another, they conclusively and hopelessly fail.   It may cost us much or it may cost us little to reach that point, but it is inevitably to be reached.   It may be after long and costly civil war, or longer and more costly foreign wars, or it may be peaceably, sensibly, and soon, but it must come.   The annexation of Cuba, international fugitive slave laws,[1] the African slave trade, judgments of the Supreme Court, and whatever else may be first asked and given, will not prevent it—nothing the North will do, nothing the North can do will prevent it.   The proximity of a people who cannot hold labor in

[1] From the *Columbia* (S. C.) *Times,* quoted without dissent in the conservative South Carolina paper, the *Charleston Mercury:*

" The loss that the South annually sustains by the running of slaves into Canada, is of sufficient importance to justify her public men in insisting upon some action of the Government of the United States in the premises.   And we confess our surprise that Southern statesmen have submitted with so much patience to the annual robbery of thousands of dollars worth of property to which she has as good a right, as the land they cultivate.   The time is propitious for the acquisition of all disputed rights from European powers.   They cannot afford to break just now with the United States.   Let our public men move in the matter, and we question not but that the President and the American Minister at St. James will give the movement a cordial support.   Besides, this is a golden moment which may never return.   Before we get another sound man in the presidential chair, peace may be made in Europe and the European powers be less inclined to look with favor upon the demands of America."

contempt ; who cannot keep laborers in ignorance and
permanent dependence each upon another man ; who
cannot have an effective censorship of the press, or a
trustworthy army of *mouchards*, prevents, and must
always prevent, the South from standing with the
slightest confidence of safety on that policy which it
proclaims to be its only ground of safety. Nothing
but a reversal of the current of our Northern history
for half a century, nothing in fact but the enslavement
of labor at the North, could in the nature of things, give
that security, even temporarily, to the capitalists of
labor at the South which they need.[1]

Some demand of the South upon the nation, acquies-
cence in which it holds essential to its safety, must then
at length be distinctly refused. And when, ten or
twenty years hence, if so be, this shall come to pass,
what then is to happen us ?

Dissolution ?

This is what many Southern politicians avow, whenever they contemplate such a contingency.

Why ?

Because it is known that the people of the North are

[1] "While it is far more obvious that negroes should be slaves
than whites, for they are only fit to labor, not to direct ; yet the
principle of slavery is itself right, and does not depend upon
difference of complexion. Difference of race, lineage, of language, of habits, and customs, all tend to render the institution
more natural and durable ; and although slaves have been generally whites, still the masters and slaves have generally been
of different national descent. Moses and Aristotle, the earliest
historians, are both authorities in favor of this difference of
race, but not of color."—*Richmond Enquirer*.

unwilling that the Union should be dissolved, whereas
they have no indisposition to the only course which it
will then be possible for the South to adopt, for the sake
of increasing the security of its citizens, against the insurrectionary movements of its slaves.   This plainly
would be to arrange a systematic opportunity and
method for the slaves to labor, whenever they chose,
and as much as they might choose, in an orderly, peaceable, and wise way, for their own release and improvement, each man for himself and those most dear to him;
each man by himself, independently, openly, with no
occasion for combination, secrecy, plots, or conspiracy.
To prepare, for those disposed to avail themselves of it,
a field, either here or elsewhere, in which their capability and Godlike reason, such as it may be, little or
great, need not be forced by law to rust unused, or
brighten *only* to the material advantage of a master.
This I must think to be consciously, even now, the
only final course of safety before every reflective Southern mind.   This, or——dissolution, and the chances of
war.

Which will be chosen?
Which is chosen?
The gambling propensity is always strong with those
who, like the wealthy Southerners, leave the details of
their business wholly to others, and who, seldom taking
the trouble to reckon beyond next year's crop, are frequently in want of occupation of mind.   Gambling is a
prevalent vice at the South.   It assumes all forms, and

it is not to be wondered at that some intelligent men,
feeling this to be true which I have said, are willing,
with their eyes open, to stake their fortunes on the
chances of war. Whatever comes of it, the leaders
would probably be able to make terms for themselves.
These intelligent men, if they can be leaders, are ready
with their stakes—other men, who do not think so far,
dissatisfied with the hand they have, are willing to try
a new shuffle. In the quadrennial howl for dissolution,
hosts of other intelligent men may unite, because it
helps, or is supposed to help, to force the North to yield
whatever may be the specific demand of the South at
the time, whether it be for a measure or a man an-
tecedent to a measure. There remains, then, the larger
part of the population, poor, ignorant people, whose
condition could not be made worse by a war. They
have nothing to sell; they buy nothing; they have
nothing which an enemy would want; nothing to fear
from devastation. At best they are indifferent. Add
to these a number of wrongheaded rich men, for want
of occupation also leads to impracticable and imagina-
tive thinking, and this invariably, with cultivated men,
to dogmatism and wrongheadedness, and we have the
elements of strength for disunion at the South—elements, it must be admitted, of a strong party, because,
for the present, nobody can experience direct harm
from it.

The substantial, intelligently occupied men, the busy,
industrious, improving poor men, form the dormant
union party. It will cohere and quicken never sooner

than is necessary to re-establish what alone now gives any degree of confidence to industrial undertakings dependent on the labor of slaves, or the demand which arises therefrom. What its strength is likely to be when the question of union or separation comes to be a practical and immediate question, will depend mainly on what the people of the South then perceive to be their highest interest. How they will then look at it, can, I think, be predicted with some confidence. Let us consider some of the probable consequences of separation or dissolution.

I couple the chances of war with disunion, not because I think no State or number of States have the abstract right to peaceably secede from the confederation, but because no possible motive can be imagined for such a secession which does not involve a state of war. It is not a negative the South wants. The threat of disunion is used only to compel the North to yield or undertake something to which the North must be disinclined. Withdraw Southern representatives from our Congress, release us from our constitutional obligations, and how are the demands of the South to be enforced except by arms? What would the South have of honor, or safety, or profit, out of the Union that she has not in it, except it were obtained by arms? I never heard the question of disunion referred to at the South, that it was not assumed to involve something of war, assumed to be in itself a demonstration of war—war to compel the North to give better protection, better profit to property in slaves. An argument for disunion is always an argu-

ment *ad hominem ;* an appeal to the warlike impulse and
the warlike pride and confidence of the South.   When I
was in the South, there was in all classes an impression,
sometimes uttered to me with distinctness and elabora-
tion, more frequently implied, that the working agricultural class, who mainly own the land, and all the
working people, of the North, were demoralized, like
slaves, by their occupation, and disinclined as much as
they were unfitted to engage in war, and that as the
property of the rich was mainly of a destructible form,
and much of it (as factories and buildings) not of a movable character, these would all come to their knees at the
slightest appearance of invasion, and by throwing the
poor out of employment, soon compel the whole people,
not otherwise so inclined, to sue for peace on whatever
terms the South should determine that its interests required.   I know that many rather well-informed men
have this idea, and I presume it is universal with the
active disunionists.   It plainly underlies all their argu-
ments, and pervades all their demonstrations which are
not obvious gasconade.

THE MILITARY CONDITION OF THE SOUTH.

It is undoubtedly true that the Southerners, compared
with ourselves, are more ready to violence, more familiar with deadly weapons, and more accustomed to
resort to physical means of self-defence.   It is also true
that they are generally less accustomed to luxury, and
are more ready for camp life than we are.   Probably,
also, they are more generally ambitious of martial glory,

and more inclined to engage in war—especially so the
wealthy young men. The latter class have likewise
been more "accustomed to command" than the corresponding class with us, and if these conditions constitute
a warlike people, or a military people, then the Southerners have a fair claim to be so designated, and to look
upon us as, comparatively speaking, a patient, peaceable,
and materialistic people. This being so, it may still
remain a question whether a "warlike" and "military"
people is safer from the evils and dangers of war than a
people ordinarily devoted in excess to the arts and industrious occupations of peace. I believe that it is an
error to suppose that the latter, however reluctant they
may be to engage in war, however even pusillanimous
they may ordinarily appear to be, are a poor stock for
soldiers when compelled, or induced by sufficient
motive, to engage in war. How was it with the greedy,
phlegmatic, hardworking, and unambitious Hollanders
(who could afford, rather than fight, to supply a foreign
tyrant and usurper—the head of a rich empire—with
two fifths of his annual revenue) when at last roused to
resist the demands of Philip II. ? The pale weavers
withdrew reluctantly from their looms, the farmers from
their dikes, the laborers from the puddle-banks, the
boatmen from the canals, the clerks from the counting-
rooms, the haberdashers, smiths, cutlers, and cobblers,
all from their shops, took up the tools and machines of
war, enrolled themselves, disciplined themselves, drilled
early and late, and, when the shock came, stood firm
and cool as veterans, so that the inflexible Alva was

compelled to exclaim, "These men," crooked, grim, pale, peaceable plodders as they were, and were willing to be, "these men are equal to the best of soldiers," and again to acknowledge, " Never was a city defended with such skill and bravery" as the manufacturing town of Harlem, chiefly by its own operatives.[1]

How was it at our own Revolution? The characteristics of the North and South then differed only from the present in degree, as clearly appears on reading Jefferson's Notes on the Virginians.

There was probably more plodding industry and less chivalrous adventure and martial ambition in Connecticut than in any other colony. Yet when, at length, success was earned, Washington, looking back with pain upon what it cost, said: "If all had done their duty as well as the little State of Connecticut, the war would have ended long ago."[2] The people of South Carolina were probably the most warlike of all, as, for the present, we use that term. But Governor Rutledge could not even get the militia to muster in defence of their own houses. Marion did bravely with a small body of skirmishers, but confessed and bewailed the fact, that the people in general had not the spirit to defend themselves, and that the State was lost through their own stupidity and factiousness, which he attributed directly to the general enslavement of the working classes, and the ignorance, idleness, and selfishness of the free.[3] It

[1] Motley's *Dutch Republic*, pages 440, 444.
[2] Irving's *Washington*, vol. iii., p. 130.
[3] See extract, *Seaboard Slave States*, vol. ii., p. 139.

was much the same throughout the slaveholding and chivalric districts ; better in the free hill country. General Greene wrote, when in command of the Southern army, and stationed in the Carolinas, "The back-country people are brave and daring, but the people on the sea-coast are sickly, and but indifferent militia."

The independence of this country is due chiefly to the good fighting qualities of what had been its most quiet, peaceable, hard-working, and plodding citizens before the war. Since the Revolution, the real military strength of the North has never been for a moment engaged. It is its yeomanry — men who have been accustomed to labor with their own hands, who have no impatient personal ambition, and who will not leave their farms, and their shops, and their families until the demand is urgent—that a hard-pressed nation always finally depends upon. And there is nowhere else in the world so numerous, or so generally intelligent, or so every way capable a yeomanry as that of our Northern States. It was by seamen out of this class that our navy was chiefly manned during the second English war, their ordinary occupations having been interrupted by it (as those of the yeomanry proper were not), and it was precisely in the qualities of cool, deliberate, and determined application of means to ends, and of steadiness under fire, that they were found to excel even the British sailor, whose ardor, and neglect to make the most of his advantages repeatedly occasioned his defeat when engaged with them.

I will not refer to the facts of the Mexican war, be-

cause there are yet no authorities whose statements upon the details would be generally accepted. I have never conversed with an officer of the line who held the popular view of the value of the services of either the Southern or the Northern volunteers ; and I have been told by one of the comrades of the "young gentlemen of good family," who came in the ranks to Vera Cruz from Mississippi and South Carolina, and of whom we have heard so much, that the larger part were constantly in hospital while they remained, and scarcely any "stood it through." As at the Revolution, they were "sickly and but indifferent militia."

THE HABIT OF COMMAND

Professor Tucker, in a *Treatise on Political Economy*, says :

"The habit of command to which the master of slaves has been familiarized from his infancy, peculiarly fits him for many of the higher duties of civilized life. He is thus likely to be better qualified for exercising authority, both in the army and navy, and even in the civil department. It, is, perhaps, thus that the Southern States have furnished more than their proportion of those who have held the higher offices of the government."[1]

This is at the bottom identical with the aristocratic theory of government. Is it to be trusted ?

The sum of the intellectual wealth possessed by the South, if it could be measured, would undoubtedly be found small, compared with that of the North, and the

[1] *Potitical Economy for the People.* By George Tucker, formerly Representative in Congress from Virginia, and Professor of Moral Philosophy in the University of Virginia.

intellectual wealth employed in all other avocations at the South, except that of the politicians, is, I should think, not equal to that of some one of the States of the North. It would be true to say that the South employs an immensely larger proportion of its whole wealth of intellectual talent in politics than the North. Englishmen, as well as Southerners, commonly consider this to be evidence, so far as it goes, of a better state of society. In my judgment, it is quite otherwise. The talent of the North is not engrossed with politics, because it is much less required in politics than in other departments of service to the public. Our method of government has this advantage, it is less dangerous than any other. It is not a religion ; it does not form society. It is the agent of society for certain limited, and, compared with the aggregate of other business which society has in hand, extremely unimportant duties. Consider the wealth which has been developed, the talent which has been called into active use for the benefit of mankind, the convenience for comfortable and intelligent living, which have been established for the use of millions of people, through the agency of some score of the leading merchants and capitalists of the city of New York, and ask whether it would not have been a most unfortunate waste of their talent, had these men, been all their time in Congress or at European courts—at the bar or on the bench ? Fulton and Whitney alone have done ten thousand times more for the wealth and power and respectability of the South than John C. Calhoun. Two Northern railroad builders

have done more, by their individual energy and good
judgment, for the State of Georgia, during the last fifteen years, than all its politicians in a century; Mr.
Ericsson will probably have accomplished infinitely
more in the next ten years for the power of the South,
through the bravery, pride, perseverance, and inflexible
will with which he has made his invention of the caloric
engine successful, than will have resulted from the labors of all the piratico-political bullies, like Walker and
Lamar, of our generation. Is not the President of the
Illinois Central Railroad Company rightly a man of
more consequence in that State than its so entitled Governor? One is paid, I suppose, two thousand dollars a
year, the other, perhaps twenty thousand, for his services, and the intellectual wealth required to satisfactorily discharge the functions of the two offices is thus
very fairly represented. Could the talent which has
been applied to the commercial enterprise of the *London Times*, during the last fifty years, have been devoted
with half the effect upon the condition of England which
it has had, if it had been employed in Parliament?
And yet the English, being a centralized government,
touching the details of its duty only by the most tedious
processes, and encumbered with old machinery of forms
and etiquette, which would be like gloves to a type-
setter, for ordinary men of business, needs a much
greater withdrawal of talent from other offices of society than ours.

We hear from Europe much reflection upon the tendency of democratic institutions to produce corruption

in office, injustice, and violence. The examples of this country which lead to these reflections, truly show the necessities of springing nations with an echoing frontier of savage and lawless life on the one side, and a continent draining life from under hard pressure, on the other. The evidence of governmental corruption, injustice, and violence which we display (and we take no care to conceal it) is trivial compared with that which escapes from the more distinctly aristocratically governed countries of Europe in an average of twenty years. I have travelled a good deal in both continents, and I cannot doubt that, spite of the general intensity and recklessness which belongs to our position in the world, there is no country in Europe where men and women may follow personal inclinations which should be harmless, with as much freedom and safety, as, on an average, in the Free States of our Republic. I make this comparison with England with the most confidence, because I have lived there for more than a year, attentively regarding the common life of the common people.

Unquestionably there are great evils arising from the lack of talent applied to our government, from the lack of real dignity of character and respectability of attainments in many government offices, but is there not quite as much of evil to the commonwealth arising from the lack of talent and of sound judgment and severe fidelity to duty in the officers of our railroad and banking systems? What losses, what untold misery has been occasioned by the ignorance, the credulity, the want of judgment of those who have formed our railroad

system. Have ignorance and folly and carelessness
occasioned half the suffering to our citizens or to the
people of Europe in dealings with the bank, the tariff,
the sub-treasury, or any other measure of civil government or laws? If some of our policemen are loafers,
and some of our senators blackguards, how is it with
our switchmen and our editors, and in which class does
any one of us, who reads a newspaper as he speeds
upon his business, prefer to have thorough discipline and
good manners ? What we have to do on this continent
is everywhere found a heavy task ; we can't afford to
employ a heavy proportion of talent or honesty about
the little share of our business which is done at the
Capital, much less can we spare it for the State House
or City Hall.

Do I write as if it were to be conceded that the South
really did get more talent applied to government than
we do? This I by no means believe. The South sends
more " orators " to Washington than the North, and the
nuisance of Washington is "bunkum" oratory. The
South speaks more Greek at Washington than the
North. The valuable men at Washington are not
speakers of Greek or aught else, but the diggers and
builders of the committees, and the clerks of the departments, and the best of these are men trained in
habits of business by the necessities of what is called
private business, and who have been drawn directly
from this private business.

It is a pleasant habit, in which most Southerners
freely indulge, both in literature and in conversation,

to repeat phrases of the significance of that of Professor Tucker, "the habit of command to which the master of slaves has been familiarized from infancy," and it seems to be generally imagined that the unmethodical, irresponsible power of compelling negro slaves to perform menial duties, must have the effect of producing a character similar to that which obtains the instinctive respect of powerful disciplined bodies of freemen. The condition of a wealthy slaveholder has some advantages, undeniably, as a preparation for civil duties, for it insures leisure for calm study and deliberate reflection to those so inclined. If it do not also lead to idle and perverse habits of mind, to Quixotic theorizing and exciting speculations, it may produce some valuable fruit in civil public life. I can see no way in which a man's character could be much affected by it favorably for military duties. It is true that a certain kind of "commanding manners" may be acquired on the plantation; that something which may be called "self-confidence in command" may be acquired, by being personally served by slaves; but, if these be valuable, as a preparation for the duties of military officers, other qualities and attainments are not less so. The country is at no little pains to select men who possess these, or will most assuredly acquire them. Our wisest and most successful officers and statesmen have formed the system in use for this purpose, and it is probably the best in the world. It begins by annually assembling a body of young men, who are inspired with the ambition, and believe themselves well prepared and adapted to be

trained for the duties of officers, who are, moreover, approved each by a member of Congress, from among all similarly disposed in his district, as the most worthy (except a certain number, nominated by the President, and supposed to be taken in equal numbers from each part of the country, and who, for the present purpose, may be left out of account). A preliminary examination is had, and if any of those selected have not been able, before the time of life at which they are allowed to present themselves, to acquire the elements of a common school education, or if any appear physically incompetent to undertake soldierly duties, they are at once set aside. No record is kept, as I am informed by the commanding officer at West Point, of these preliminary examinations.

For four years afterwards, sometimes five, those who are found so far capable as to be worth the trouble, are kept in training and on trial for competency as soldiers and officers. Once a year the result is published, the names of a certain number, who are entitled the " most distinguished," being officially announced in the *Army Register*. So far as it has been possible to construct a rule for the measurement of the qualifications needed for military command, these young men are the best which our government, acting under the advice of our most experienced military men, has been able to obtain in the country. I have examined the *Registers* as far back as 1848, and find that in the eight years following,[1] the first distinction has been gained by twenty-

[1] Subsequent registers I had not been able to obtain when

four entered from the Free States and by two entered
from the Slave States. Of all those obtaining official honors in the same time, one hundred and
eight entered from the Free States and thirty-four
from the Slave States. Of those who, during the
same period, were either discharged, sent back, or
barely whipped through (being the lowest ten of each
class, including those thrown out) a minority of all
were from the Free States.

Certainly there are qualities of the highest value for
conducting military operations which the West Point
sifting cannot catch; and it is not impossible that the
men who have been most punctual, most exact, most
thorough, indefatigable, and tenacious in all the
opportunities there offered them to develop the most
necessary qualities and obtain the most necessary
acquirements of modern warriors may be most deficient in the native talent which overcomes that class
of difficulties for which there can be no sufficient preparation until they arise on the field. What are these
other qualities, and how can they be manifested? They
are mainly included under a single phrase—fertility of
resource ; in other words—inventive genius. How
stands the evidence as to the respective strength of the
Free and Slave States in this quality? The record at
Washington shows, in a single year, two thousand
original inventions from the Free States, established

---

this chapter was prepared. They would not alter the general
indications of these.

before the patent office examiners, to less than three hundred from the Slave States.

A very well informed writer has observed that military qualities, both as regards bravery and fitness for the work, are, upon the whole, pretty evenly distributed among the civilized nations ; that it is not so much the degree as the special nature of the qualification which distinguishes the soldiers of different nationalities—each having some advantages and disadvantages over all others.[1] It is hardly necessary to say anything of courage. It is rarely, except from want of *esprit de corps*, and, with new soldiers, faithless in their organization, that cowardice becomes an important element in determining the result of a warlike struggle. If the Southerner has more ardor and readiness for deeds of arms, if he has more personal military ambition, more dash and reckless daring, the Northerner has more stanchness, and, once roused, more untiring, sober, and trustworthy enthusiasm. If the South has the most squirrel shooters, street skirmishers, and duellists, the North has most men who have proved themselves heroes in contests with the elements, and who appreciate and are accustomed to the benefits resulting from the subordination of the individual will to the corporate. The North has also much the largest force of enrolled militia :

> North, number.... 1,381,843
> South,   "   792,876

[1] *Putnam's Monthly*, August, 1855.

A mere enrollment is of little value without organization and equipment. There is no doubt that a far larger proportion of the Northern enrolled militia is in some degree organized, equipped, drilled, and accustomed to act under its officers than of the Southern.

The comparative material resources of the two parts of our country, really the most important circumstance by which to determine their comparative ability to endure war, having been much discussed and set forth with other purposes, it is unnecessary to more than remind the reader of the entirely overwhelming power the North controls in this respect. The census returns indicate the

REAL AND PERSONAL PROPERTY :

In the Free States.......... $4,102,172,108
" Slave States (including
slaves).............. 2,936,081,731

But, for war purposes, it is certainly absurd to hold slaves at a higher valuation than free men. Considering negroes, then, as no more to be reckoned a part of the wealth of the country than other men, the comparison will stand :

REAL AND PERSONAL PROPERTY :

Free States $4,102,172,108
Slave States (slaves not included) . 1,336,090,737 [1]

The present actual revenue of the Free States is to that of the Slave States as eighteen to eight.

[1] Slaves valued at a trifle over five hundred dollars a head ; a low estimate.

The purely military resources are certainly not less preponderating in the Free States than might be presumed from these figures; the stock of saltpetre, lead, hospital stores, etc., being always far larger, and the principal manufactories of arms, vehicles, etc.—not considering those of the Government—being in the Free States.

In means of rapidly concentrating land forces, the advantage of the North is sufficiently indicated by a comparison of the extent of

COMPLETED RAILROADS :

Free States, miles (1857)........ 17,855
Slave States, miles (1857)....... 6,859

The latter being much more poorly equipped, and rarely double-tracked. The cost of the Northern roads has been more than five times those of the South.

Still more, by a comparison of the cost of transporting the mails, which is more than four times as much at the South, relatively to the amount carried, as at the North.

MAIL TRANSPORTATION—COST FOR EVERY DOLLAR
RECEIVED IN POSTAGE :

Free States............ 56 cts.
Slave States........... $1.51

As to marine resources for the purpose, more than nine tenths of all the shipping and boats of the United States (tonnage capacity) have been built, and are now owned north of the Potomac and the Ohio.

Whether the fact that a large constituent of the

working force of the South is the offspring of a subjected foreign people, itself held to labor without stipu-
lated wages, not connected by marriage with the
citizens, owning nothing of the property, having no
voice in the State, in the lowest degree ignorant, and yet
half barbarous in disposition and habits—whether this
fact is an element of strength or weakness in a civilized
war—can it be a question ?

Certainly not, in the minds of the gentlemen in our
confederate employment, who are also engaged in the
work of " preparing the South for its destiny," as the
following extracts from De Bow's *Resources of the
South* will indicate :

"If anything is certain in human affairs, it is certain, and from
the most obvious considerations, that we are more secure in this
respect than any civilized and fully peopled society on the face
of the earth.   In every such society there is a much larger proportion than with us of persons who have more to gain than to
lose by the overthrow of government and the embroiling of
social order." * * * "It is almost physically impossible
that there should be any very extensive combination among
the slaves." * * * "The efficiency of an army is determined by the quality of its officers.   And may we not hope to
have a greater number of men better qualified for officers, and
possessing the true spirit of military command." * * * "The
Helots were a regular constituent of the Spartan armies.   Thoroughly acquainted with their characters and accustomed to command them, we might use any strictness of discipline which
would be necessary to render them effective, and from their
habits of subordination already formed this would be a task of
less difficulty." * * * "With white officers, *and accom-
panied by strong white cavalry*, there are no troops in the world
from which there would be so little reason to apprehend insubordination or mutiny."

The opinion here indicated that the slaves are a

thoroughly subjected race, that they recognize and quail instinctively before their masters, is a correct one, generally speaking, as I have often noticed ; but that this "instinct"—that is to say, instinct-like habit of mind—can be depended upon at all times is far from being true, as also I have seen abundant evidence. Let the negro have a strong scent of freedom, and how the real instinct of manhood, which has been lying dormant perhaps for generations, may chance to take possession of him, the editor of the *Feliciana Whig* (Louisiana newspaper), with the simple eloquence of a pure savage, shall testify :

"On Saturday last, a runaway negro was killed in the parish of East Baton Rouge, just below the line of this parish, under the following circumstances: Two citizens of Port Hudson, learning that a negro was at work on a flatboat, loading with sand, just below that place, who was suspected of being a runaway, went down in a skiff for the purpose of arresting him.

"Having seized him and put him into the skiff they started back, but had not proceeded far when the negro, who had been at the oars, seized a hatchet and assaulted one of them, wounding him very seriously. A scuffle ensued, in which both parties fell overboard. They were both rescued by the citizen pulling to them with the skiff. Finding him so unmanageable, the negro was put ashore, and the parties returned to Port Hudson for arms and a pack of negro dogs, and started again with the intention to capture him. They soon got on his trail, and when found again he was standing at bay upon the outer edge of a large raft of drift wood, armed with a club and pistol.

"In this position he bade defiance to men and dogs—knocking the latter into the water with his club, and resolutely threatening death to any man who approached him. Finding him obstinately determined not to surrender, one of his pursuers shot him. He fell at the third fire, and so determined was he not to be captured, that when an effort was made to rescue him from drowning he made battle with his club, and sunk waving his

weapon in angry defiance at his pursuers. He refused to give the name of his owner." [1]

So far as I could ascertain, there are but few districts in which, ordinarily, insurrection is much or constantly, at present, apprehended. Yet there is no part of the South where the slave population is felt to be quite safe from a contagion of insurrectionary excitement. Any great event having the slightest bearing upon the question of emancipation is known to produce an " unwholesome excitement," even in parts of the country where the slave population is, and has least reason not to be, peculiarly contented with its condition. The last presidential election was followed by the discovery of conspiracies and insurrectionary symptoms in all but, I believe, three of the Slave States. It was estimated at the time that, altogether, not less than sixty slaves were put to death ; some by hanging, but many by torture, in the efforts to check the supposed contagion of revolt. The danger seemed at this time to be about equal in the

[1] That the reader may appreciate more perfectly the condition of the soul which could describe in these terms such a glory of mankind as this nigger, who—by the grace of God, a true nobleman—made and kept himself a free man, I quote from Norman's *New Orleans and its Environs*, an account of the leading class of Feliciana:

" This latter received its beautiful and expressive name from its beautifully variegated surface of hills and valleys, and its rare combination of all the qualities that are most desired in a planting country. It is a region of almost fairy beauty and wealth. Here are some of the wealthiest and most intelligent planters and the finest plantations in the State, the region of princely taste and more than patriarchal hospitality," etc.

It is the region and the people, in short, I described in the first chapter of this volume [vol. i.].

farming and in the planting districts. In but one or two of those districts in which the danger is ordinarily considered greatest, did evidence of unusual excitement among the slaves become public, undoubtedly because, in those districts, the precautions had been strenuous and sufficient—that is to say, because the white population was vigilant, and the slaves felt themselves under a strong hand.

An armed citizens' police, having a military organization, is, as I have before said, sustained in all parts of the South where there are many slaves. It is more or less efficient according to the necessities of the case, but any long continued entire neglect usually results in general insubordination and much inconvenience, as is indicated in the following remarks upon a robbery in his neighborhood by a Texas editor:

" While all the men were gone from the place, a negro described as being bare-headed, thick-set, and having on a blue blanket coat and a pair of blue cottonade pants, came to the house, and seeing a double-barrel gun in the corner took it. He then ordered Mrs. Krouse to get him some ammunition, threatening to kill her if she refused. Having got this, he warned her to make no alarm or he would come back and shoot her down. He then made the best of his way off.

" We can but say in connection with this affair that the patrols of the various parts of the country are getting to be lamentably lax in their duty. There are at this time at least a dozen runaway negroes that we know of in the county. We hear of thieveries committed by them every day or two. The above is the boldest act we have yet heard of, and yet that may be followed by yet bolder ones, if this state of things is not checked. When it comes to this, that our property is not secure in our houses, in broad daylight, from the incursions of these vagabonds, and that even the lives of defenseless women are threatened by them,

it is time something was done. Let the captains of the patrol look to their duty."

It must be borne in mind that throughout the South slaves are accustomed to "run away." On every large or moderate plantation which I visited, I had evidence that in peace, with, south of Virginia and east of Texas, no prospect of finding shelter within hundreds of miles, or of long avoiding recapture and severe punishment, many slaves had a habit of frequently making efforts to escape temporarily from their ordinary condition of subjection. I have shown that this is so common that Southern writers gravely describe it as a disease — a monomania, to which the negro race is peculiarly subject, making the common mistake of attributing to blood that which is much more rationally to be traced to condition.

This is the difference between slave and other property. Ships, goods, buildings, machinery, stores may be destroyed, and to some extent, with labor and hazard, carried off. Hence those interested to maintain these things are most anxious to prevent invasion—to annoy and check the progress of invaders by any available means. Slaves may carry themselves off, and with themselves may carry off much other property, which, under ordinary circumstances of war, is not accessible by an enemy. When a slave now runs for the frontier, he seldom neglects the attempt to despoil his master, in some way or other, of movable property, justifying himself with himself on the ground that he has earned wages which have been withheld from him. In a

large proportion of all cases, Texas runaways are advertised as having taken a horse, a gun, money, and clothes.

To suppose that in case of a war, either foreign or civil, the slaves would be an element of strength to the South, or that an enemy could not easily turn them to account, seems to me to be, on the face of it, a foundation upon which only the maddest theorist or the most impracticable of abstractionists could found a policy. Whether, finally, in case of the civil war with a threat of which we have so often been threatened, and the periodical suggestion of which will, in the ordinary course of events, soon be presented to us again, Northern men are likely to be more influenced by the cost of extra-hazardous insurance policies on their manufactures and stores, than Southern gentlemen by the dread of losing the services of their slaves, we can best judge by reference to the past.

During the Revolution, the British ships on the coast, at times offered protection to runaway slaves ; and it was estimated that they carried away from Virginia alone not less than thirty thousand of them.[1] Washington demanded the restoration of one hundred and fifty taken at one time to Nova Scotia, which was refused by Sir Guy Carleton.[2] John Jay, writing to John Adams, says : "Great numbers of slaves were carried away by the British forces from other ports beside New York."[3] In the second English war, the enemy had

[1] Hildreth, vol. iii., p. 355.
[2] Sparks's *Dip. Cor.*, vol. iv., p. 173. [3] *Ibid.*, p. 358.

too few ships to spare, and little opportunity to adopt
the same means of annoyance; but a proclamation of
Admiral Cochrane in the spring of 1814, caused great
alarm at the South, it being addressed to the slaves,
under the denomination " of all persons desirous to
emigrate from the United States." These were informed that they would receive protection on board any
of his majesty's ships, and be given free passage to free
soil, if they desired it.[1] A large sum was afterwards
claimed as indemnity for slaves so carried away, and
the claim referred to Russia as arbiter.[2]

The testimony of Mr. Madison, given in a debate in
Congress, 1797, on a proposition to impose a duty upon
the importation of slaves,[3] is as follows :

" It is to be hoped that by expressing a natural disapproba-
tion of this trade we may destroy it, and save ourselves from
reproaches, and our posterity the imbecility ever attendant on a
country filled with slaves.   I do not wish to say anything harsh
to the hearing of gentlemen who entertain different sentiments
from me, or different sentiments from those I represent, but if
there is any one point in which it is clearly the policy of this
nation, so far as we constitutionally can, to vary the practice obtaining under some of the State governments, it is this.   But it
is certain a majority of the States are opposed to this practice,
therefore, upon principle, we ought to discountenance it as far
as it is in our power.

" If I were not afraid of being told that the representatives
of the several States are the best able to judge of what is proper
and conducive to their particular prosperity, I should venture
to say that it is as much the interest of Georgia and South Carolina as of any in the Union. *Every addition they receive to
their number of slaves tends to weaken and render them less*

---

[1] Hildreth, vol. vi., p. 483.   [2] *Ibid.*, p. 660.
[3] Barton's *Debates*, p. 75.

*capable of self-defense. In case of hostilities with foreign nations,
they will be the means of inviting attack instead of repelling
invasion.* It is the necessary duty of the general government
to protect every part of the empire against danger, as well internal as external. Everything, therefore, which tends to
increase this danger, though it may be a local affair, yet if it involves national expense or safety, becomes of concern to every
part of the Union, and is a proper subject for the consideration of those charged with the general administration of the
government."

The most conclusive evidence, however, is that given
by that sound and clear-headed patriot, Marion, whose
words in reply to De Kalb's inquiry, why the South
Carolinians were all "running to take British protec-
tions," I again quote :

"We told him the reason was very plain to us who were inhabitants of that country, and knew very well the state of things
there. * * * The people of Carolina form two classes, the rich
and the poor. The poor are generally very poor, because not
being necessary to the rich, who have slaves to do all the work,
they get no employment of them. Being thus unsupported by
the rich, they continue poor and low-spirited. They seldom
get money, and, indeed, what little they do get is laid out in
brandy to raise their spirits, and not on books and newspapers
to get information. Hence, they know nothing of the comparative blessings of our country or of the dangers which threaten it,
and, therefore, care nothing about it. As to the other class, the
rich, they are very rich, and consequently, *afraid to stir, unless
a fair chance offer, lest the British should burn their houses
and furniture, and carry off their negroes and stock.*"

And South Carolina is far weaker on these grounds
to-day than she was at the Revolution. So is all the
cotton region. The border States on the North are
possibly stronger, but if English ships drew slaves
from their masters to be transported to Nova Scotia,

what would England itself brought along side of Virginia have done?

Chancellor Harper, of South Carolina, after claiming that there would be less danger from insubordination of the slaves if the South were engaged in war, than usual, because there would then be a larger force of armed men a-foot within the country than usual, by which they would be overawed, urges that it is practicable and may be found best to put arms in the hands of the slaves themselves and lead them against the enemy, but concludes that if this were attempted it might be dangerous, after a peace had again been obtained, to attempt to reduce them "to their former condition of laborers." " It might be necessary," he says, " when once embodied, to keep them so, and subject to military discipline—a permanent standing army. This, in time of peace, would be expensive, if not dangerous."

Few Northern readers can read this conclusion, reflecting that the contingency it supposes is coolly discussed as one of the probable necessities of a severe campaign of war by one of the oftest-quoted authorities of the extreme Southern party, and hold the common sense of the South in so little respect as to apprehend that an actual fighting war has ever been contemplated in earnest as a means of strengthening slavery. They will be more likely to believe, that while a war-like demonstration is intended, nothing like a war in earnest is presumed by those whose voice renders the threat of secession worthy of our notice. This is my own judgment. With few exceptions—madder enthusiasts than any we

can set against them—these men pledge, and swear, and solemnly vow themselves to the alternative of secession, in the belief that should the presumed condition arise, and should they be forced to attempt to fulfil their vows, commercial interests, under the instant check to trade which would occur at the first demonstration of arms, would prevail, the North recede, and a new confederate constitution be obtained, giving new national securities for slavery.

This error is to be attributed to the prevalent opinion of the South, by which the most intelligent must be affected, that labor begets pusillanimity, and commercial habits unfitness for war, and hence that a real danger of war would bring the South the immediate moral support of a host of people who now resist the demands of the South.

The fact is, that the native rural population of the North is a peculiarly law-loving, and, in this way, a peace-loving people ; the strength of the party which the South has agreed to deal with as an enemy is mainly with this class of people.   That party can, in the nature of things, never undertake to accomplish its purposes by illegal or unconstitutional acts without losing the support of a large proportion of the rural voters of the North.

Whatever their personal views may be, the leaders of the free soil army of the North know this, and will be governed as politicians and as statesmen by it.   On the other hand, no party could exist in an effective form for political action at the North, which supported

men who were avowedly acting disloyally to the constitution at the South. A secession movement at the
South, based on anything but an unquestionable act
of unconstitutional aggression against the South, would
then, as soon as it began to be regarded with respect at
the North, find few apologists, no practical supporters.
Long before it brought about a serious passage of arms,
the North would be practically united in one party
against it, and in support of the government to which
it was opposed. Evidence of this would alone be necessary to convince any intelligent man at the South of
the folly of the attempt to coerce the North, and of the
necessity for the adoption at home of a new policy—a
policy by which the South should no longer depend
upon the co-operation of the North in providing against
the dangers of slavery. Of necessity, the reactionary
party would represent and embody the strength of
the nation, that is to say, of the entire North added to
itself, in carrying out its policy. Thus, I see no cause
for alarm, but only for hope of a peaceful end to our
great national squabble, in the most violent and solemn
determination for dissolution and war which can be
exhibited at the South.

As the present policy so madly pursued has departed
from the principles of Democracy and the old Democratic party, so that the words of Jefferson would now
hang a man anywhere at the South, I do not much
doubt that when reaction comes, the principles on which
Jefferson desired to deal with slavery will be found eminently safe and profitable. There would still be ex-

tremists ; there would be fanatics and fools ; there would
be great difference of opinion as to the ultimate destiny
of the negro race, and as to the final disappearance of
slavery, and difference of judgment among moderate
men as to measures ; but the common sense of the South
would be seconded by the common sense of the North,
and would receive the respect of the world, when it had
established a policy the tendency of which would be to
encourage slaves to form industrious habits and exercise intelligence, by securing them palpable benefits
therefrom ; which would discourage idleness and im-
providence, as well as other vices, by punishments
which they would dread, making grades, perhaps, from
the utterly low slave upward, to what rank here, those
governing would determine, but to freedom and the
most complete fair play somewhere else if not here ;
and every step upward, an object to be desired by those
below ; every lapse through the vices of slavery, or the
weaknesses alleged of the negro nature, distinctly and
surely to be apprehended disagreeably.   And together
with this, the encouragement of denser and more completely furnished communities of citizens.   (Jefferson
proposed to the constitutional convention of Virginia to
give free passage, and offer special inducements to
whites to come to Virginia).

It will be said, of course, that however practicable in
Jefferson's time, nothing of this kind is so now, since
the demand for cotton has quadrupled the value of
slaves.   It is for this reason now practicable, if not before.   There is no slave so valuable that he could not

make himself more valuable if he knew how, and chose
to be more valuable. Increase his industry and intelligence, and he becomes more valuable. Punish him
as now, but more systematically and effectually for laziness, stupidity, and carelessness, but hold before him a
sure reward for industry, study of his allotted duty, and
perseverance in it, and he will share all the larger
interests of his master, and be equally anxious with him
for the suppression of disorder in lower and more
vicious classes than his own. There is many a negro
who is now considered a dangerous, or at least a "rascally" fellow, whose labor brings not four bales of cotton a year, who, if he saw hard fare and a well organized and thorough penal system on one side, and freedom, or a sure progress toward it for himself and his
family on the other, with luxuries meanwhile, could
and would make his labor worth as much as seven
bales of cotton a year. In half a dozen years, the difference would be equal to his present value. At the
same time, his personal interest at stake in the maintenance of the existing system of government, and of
peace and order, would be yearly and daily increasing.

The task method of working slaves which prevails in
much of South Carolina and Georgia, proves, in my
judgment, that what would seem the most serious difficulty in such a system amounts to nothing, when self-
interest is once felt to be engaged in its success, for the
common overseers, men who cannot read and write
themselves, allot the tasks to the slaves, and seldom fail

to have them executed.[1]   On the other hand, where
the system has once been established, it is found very
difficult and not very profitable, to force the slaves to
work more for their master than the custom.   Give
custom the sanction and penalties of law, and let the
community feel its peace to be endangered by a disregard of the law, and there would be certainly less
knavery and cruelty to the negro than now; more
wealth with less care to the master.

[1] See *Seaboard Slave States*, vol. ii., p. 62–76.

INDEX

A

Abington, II., 26
Abolition in Tennessee, II., 25; publishers, II., 239
Abolitionism, II., 30
Abolitionist, a Mississippi slaveholding, I., 196; –207
Absenteeism, I., 128, 175
Agriculture in northern Virginia, II., 28
Agriculturist, The Southern, extract from, I., 57,69
Alabama tradesman, I., 52
Aristocratic "swell-heads," I., 25–26, 35–36
Arms carrying, I., 24
Asheville, I., 280; II., 1

B

Bacon raising, I., 47
Bakersville, 20
Balsam Mountain, II., 2; scenery, 7
Barton, Dr., quoted, II., 110–111, 161
Beasts of prey in highlands, I., 251
Big Black River, I., 59
Bill of fare, I., 138
"Blackleg" gentleman, I., 143
"Black, White and Yellow," I., 93
Books, dangerous, II., 237
Branding, I., 276
Brandon Republican, extract from, II., 40

Breeding slaves for sale in the South, II., 189; degeneracy of, 203
Brooks, P. S., and Mr. Sumner, II., 226
Business men, "important to," I., 9

C

Calhoun Institute, I., 17
California slaves, II., 17
Camp-meeting, I., 144
Cartwright, Prof., quoted, I., 98; II., 220
Census of 1850, extract from, I., 105; returns of property, II., 260
Charleston, S. C., *Standard,* extracts from, II., 41, 133; *Mercury,* extracts from, II., 130, 132–133
Children, I., 198–199
Christian duty of the North, II., 25
Church edifices, value of, I., 106–107
Clay, Cassius, II., 165
Climate of the back highlands, I., 247; of Louisiana bottom-lands, II., 109
Clothing of slaves, I., 81–82
Colonization, an advocate of, II., 15; slavery, a system of, 47
Color, I., 93, 208
Congo "niggers," II., 220
Connecticut, proverbial meanness, II., 182; hospitality, 182

277